About the author:

Stephanie Dowrick has been actively interested in
psychotherapy since the late 1970s. She has training in
analytic psychotherapy and psychosynthesis as well as Gestalt
therapy and individual and marital counselling. To the
creation of her self-help books, she also brings extensive
publishing and writing experience.

She began work in the publishing industry in 1972 and was
co-founder and Managing Director of The Women's Press
from 1977 to 1982. In 1991 she was appointed Chairwoman
of The Women's Press.

Stephanie has been writing professionally since 1983. Her
work includes a novel, *Running Backwards Over Sand*, as
well as *Intimacy and Solitude* – an immediate international
bestseller – and *The Intimacy and Solitude Self-Therapy
Book*. She has combined writing her books with publishing
and teaching writing and, more recently, with running a
private psychotherapy practice and giving group workshops.

Stephanie Dowrick was born in New Zealand, lived in Europe
for much of her adult life, and is now based in Sydney,
Australia, where she has a son and a daughter.

About *Intimacy and Solitude*:

'Not simply another manual for solving your life in ten easy lessons. Sympathetically and with a rare clarity, it offers penetrating insights into some of the most basic paradoxes of human relationships.' *Guardian*

'A blockbusting study which encompasses and attempts to unravel the politics, psychology and spirituality of close relationships.' *The Scotsman*

'Penetrating, thoroughly researched, thoughtful and thought-provoking . . . Don't stay home on your own without it.' *Everywoman*

'I opened it and found myself hooked. Here was an analysis of close relationships which struck home, readable but not over-simplistic, based on informed research and extensive interviews. You don't have to agree with it all to appreciate its exposition of the social pressures which go into forming our view of ourselves.' *Sun-Herald*

'Genuinely illuminating of the business of understanding oneself and others. It is by turns intelligent, eloquent and wise.' *Metro*

Also by Stephanie Dowrick from The Women's Press:

Why Children? with Sibyl Grundberg (1980)
Intimacy and Solitude (1992)

STEPHANIE DOWRICK

THE
intimacy & solitude
SELF-THERAPY
BOOK

Published in Great Britain by
The Women's Press Ltd, 1993
A member of the Namara Group
34 Great Sutton Street, London EC1V 0DX

First published in Australia by William Heinemann,
Australia, 1993
A division of Reed International Books
Australia Pty Ltd

British Library Cataloguing-in-Publication Data
Dowrick, Stephanie
  Intimacy and Solitude Self-therapy Book
  I. Title
  158.2

ISBN 0 7043 4377 0

Typeset in 10/13 Garamond Roman

Printed and bound in Great Britain by
Cox and Wyman Ltd, Reading, Berks

For Niki Honoré and Susanne Kahn-Ackermann

May we all come home to our completeness.

Contents

demands; Your significant others are separate people; The rewards of negative emotions; 'I am not my negative emotions'; Observing your anger; 'I am entitled to my anger because . . .'; Not rage, but . . .; Hurling your anger into the ocean of life; Intimate listening; Listening with awareness; 'I can't listen'; Saying no to listening; Speak for yourself; Understanding, not advice; Saying no; Alone and together; Attack and reconciliation; Refusing negative projections; Avoiding suspicion; When is a relationship over?; Separating—and learning; How to avoid fights!

Introduction; In the eyes of my ideal lover I am . . .; Meditation on love (1); Meditation on love (2); From fear to love; Focus on the present; Trust; Who is in charge of your life?; An affirmation of self-worth; What's missing?; Life is unfair; Asking for what you want; Not getting what you want; Refusing others what they want; Moving from wanting to needing; Wants and needs in conflict; Filling the sky with hot-air balloons; Not wanting—having!; Applying the magical balm; Journey through your body; When sexual desire fades or dies; I am no longer sexually desiring; I am no longer sexually desired; Reversing roles; Giving sexual desire the kiss of life; Reviewing your day; Reviewing the day with children; Listening. Just listening; Measure your life with a piece of string; Conscious choosing.

About this book's foundations

I would like to acknowledge that I could not have written this *Self-Therapy Book*, nor found the courage to try, without my knowledge of psychosynthesis, an approach to psychotherapy which arose in response to Freudian psychoanalysis. Roberto Assagioli, psychosynthesis's founding father, was more or less contemporary with Freud and was himself one of Italy's first analysts, but he believed that many people need a psychotherapeutic approach which explicitly honours and supports their search for life's meaning and for higher values alongside psychological and social understanding.

A few of the active meditations included here derive from Roberto Assagioli's own inspired portfolio. But the optimistic stance of the *Self-Therapy Book* as a whole—its belief in the innate goodness of human beings; its trust that you have an inner world worth exploring; its inclusiveness of 'meaning of life' questions; its attention to the resonances between our inner and outer worlds: this all reflects the stance of psychosynthesis.

'Psychosynthesis provides a philosophy that aims to reach both the id and the Self,' suggests Frank Haronian. 'Psychosynthesis aims to help [us] recognise all of [our] impulses, to accept the responsibility of deciding which to express and which to renounce, and to deal with the anxiety that is an inescapable aspect of the process of self-actualisation.'

In *Psychosynthesis Counselling in Action*, Diana Whitmore puts it even more simply: 'Psychosynthesis counselling is based on a vision of human life which confronts pain and neuroses but within the wider context of evoking and strengthening that which is good, right and beautiful.'

Those who would like to further their experience of psychosynthesis are directed towards Diana's book, and also to *What We May Be* by Piero Ferrucci, which I continue to recommend without reservation.

I also want to pay full-hearted tribute to the work of Sheila Ernst and Lucy Goodison. In the late 1970s I edited and then published at The Women's Press their book, *In Our Own Hands: A Book of Self-Help Therapy*. I worked with Lucy and Sheila over several years that were rich for us all. But much as I loved working with them, and as much as I learned from them, I had no idea how the work on that book would affect me personally, and what part it would play in setting me off on my own vocational path.

Lastly, as I was doing the final draft on this manuscript, I was given Thich Nhat Hanh's *Peace Is Every Step*. There I found my own work with aware breathing raised to an art, beautiful in its simplicity. I have borrowed his 'Breathing in I calm my body. Breathing out I smile' for my life and for these pages.

Acknowledgements

My thanks to all the people who have written to me, phoned in to radio programmes when I was speaking, attended workshops or public events, or have otherwise taken the trouble to tell me how my earlier book, *Intimacy and Solitude*, is affecting their lives. I have been touched and glad—and inspired by you to write this book of self-therapy.

My loving thanks, too, to my family, friends and therapists for inspiration, patience and trust, and an easing of my life as I have written this book: especially my beloved children Gabriel and Kezia Dowrick, their father Ric Sissons, Janice Daw, Sally Gillespie, Robin Hundt, Geraldine Killalea, Jocelyn Krygier, Neil Phillips and Julie Steiner.

Thanks, too, to my own psychotherapy clients who allow me to share their discovery and unfolding of secrets and processes of change. I learn so much from you.

Lucy Goodison read an earlier version of the text and gave me a detailed, knowledgeable response which allowed me to see weaknesses and develop strengths in a way I could never have done alone. Whatever faults the book still has, it is much clearer for Lucy's interventions. I am immensely grateful. Such weaving of Lucy's work with my own has a long, rewarding history. I regard it as one of my life's graces.

Kathy Gale of The Women's Press also read that earlier draft and made some invaluable politically minded suggestions. For those, too, I am most grateful.

To Kath Downie at Reed Publishing in New Zealand, many thanks for all that you have done with the most delightful enthusiasm. A special thanks to Sue Hines and Fran Berry at Reed Books in Australia for your lively and productive engagement with the *Intimacy and Solitude* project. Thanks, too, to the sales representatives in both New Zealand and Australia, my two home countries. Without your support *Intimacy and Solitude* could not have soared, and this self-therapy book might have gone unwritten. Let me sing your praises!

The author and the publishers also wish to thank Shekinah Creative Ministry for permission to use part of Noël Davis' poem, 'Love's Silent Song'; Ingram Smith for his permission to use the passage from *Truth is a Pathless Land* which is reproduced here as 'Listening. Just listening'; and Lauris Edmond for the lines from her poem, 'Love Poem'.

When we open our eyes, we see beyond ourselves.
When we open our ears, we listen beyond ourselves.
When we surrender to this attraction, we grow in self-awareness.

Wisdom from the Elders of the Senecas

Self-Therapy

Introduction

The *Intimacy and Solitude Self-Therapy Book* offers you a fresh, creative way to think about emotional problems and hurdles. It guides you as you locate and open doors in blank walls; it offers support and inspiration as alternatives to self-defeat or despair.

The *Self-Therapy Book* offers that support in a way which is direct and uncluttered.

It encourages you to develop a life-enhancing relationship with your own inner world. It is this infinitely rich relationship that will allow you to discover much about your life alone and with others in the present, and to face and explore the relationships which haunt you from the past.

- Healing old wounds
- knowing what limits and drives you
- creating new choices
- increasing the subtlety of your interactions with others
- dismantling the apparatus of your own limitations
- growing in self-acceptance
- experiencing yourself actively in the world outside yourself.

These would be legitimate goals of any form of therapy, and are the goals of the self-therapy made available here.

The *Self-Therapy Book* develops two simple yet profound capacities:

1 To ask questions which will reveal your inner world to you.
2 To bring conscious awareness to the life you want to be living.

Writing the *Self-Therapy Book*, I have assumed that you function emotionally, intellectually and spiritually at a level of complexity that is often difficult to make sense of on your own.

Where do you begin in the quest to understand yourself and others more deeply? How do you recognise limiting patterns of feeling or behaviour? Why does your behaviour fall short of your intentions? How should you put into practice new insights and discoveries? This book helps you shape and respond to those questions and many others *in your own way*, and to make discoveries appropriate to yourself and the world around you, *at your own pace*.

There is a strong focus here on the positive and the possible. This is not to deny or trivialise the pain that is part of most people's lives, but accepting pain—even experiencing it fully— can allow you a more inclusive view of your life.

Equally, while you will come to know your personal history more deeply, there is less emphasis on the past than there might be within the safety of a therapeutic relationship. Here the emphasis is on living in the present—with heightened awareness and fresh resolve.

Writing, day-dreaming, taking guided journeys inwards, drawing images from your unconscious onto the page, becoming newly aware of your body and especially your breathing: these activities are crucial to this approach to self-therapy, with a constant renewal of creativity through 'thinking in pictures'.

'Thinking in pictures . . . approximates more closely to unconscious processes than does thinking in words,' wrote Sigmund Freud in *The Ego and the Id*. Thinking in pictures is a skill this self-therapy allows you to develop quickly. Working with symbolic images, you can bypass many of your limiting patterns of think-ing. You can also reach backwards and forwards to discoveries that exist without and beyond words.

These active meditations expand your awareness of past and present, of thoughts and feelings, of memory and creativity. They develop your courage to think, feel, dream and act in ways that are true to who you most deeply wish to be. They develop self-love, self-acceptance and self-knowledge.

And this approach to self-therapy does not stop with 'self'. There is no retreat from engagement with people, social issues, local and planetary concerns. On the contrary, these active medita-tions can give you the confidence and the means to increase that vital (and vitalising) capacity emphasised in *Intimacy and Solitude*: **to put yourself imaginatively in the place of someone else, to know what that person is feeling, and to believe their feelings matter.** But that cannot happen while you remain your own biggest mystery, or while you feel ruled by self-doubt or self-denigration.

Increasing self-love as you increase your love for others; increas-ing self-knowledge as you come to 'read' others with greater subtlety; accepting yourself as you come to accept others as they are, and not only as you would like them to be: these are self-therapy challenges which can—and perhaps must—take place simultaneously if they are to have any lasting meaning.

Do those seem like awesome goals to you? Yet I know from my own therapy, and from working and sharing with others, that they are not unrealistic. Nevertheless, it was obviously a delicate and sometimes daunting task to take what is possible within the intimacy of a therapeutic relationship and bring that alive on the page. What's more, in *Intimacy and Solitude* I clearly stated that I do not like psychological recipe books; that I do not think they can be more than briefly useful. So, writing this *Self-Therapy Book*, I have been conscious that for all its necessarily guided active meditations and exercises, I would need to avoid the recipe book approach.

What I have attempted here is structured but highly flexible encouragement to enter and take seriously the inner world of your own psyche. Doing so, you will understand and unravel psychological questions or crises, and move towards healing and forgiving *in the way you need*. You will learn not from my instructions *but from what the meditations allow you to discover about your own experiences and desires*.

Thus, when stress and pain and conflict arise—as they inevitably will throughout your life—they can be experienced as part of life, without your resorting to the denial or avoidance of pain which leaves so many people depressed, numb, confused, drugged or dead. Working with self-therapy, you will find yourself able to encompass pain and remain open to pleasure—not because I have solved your problems for you, but because you have the means to find the necessary wisdom within yourself, however out of touch with those resources you may at this moment feel.

In their variety, the self-therapy approaches of this book combine most positively to stretch your capacities for thinking *and* feeling *and* acting with good will. What's more, as you open to self-therapy, you will find inspiration from other sources: from books concerned with psychological or spiritual matters; from people whose quest to understand life beyond the superficialities matches your own.

As new insights almost literally tumble into your life, self-therapy will seem stimulating and exciting. (It can also be slow, demanding and easy to avoid doing!) But even at its most exhilarating, self-therapy is not a matter of increased intellectual insight only. Your intellect can and will be your ally, but while an expansion of conscious awareness embraces mind, it is not confined to mind only. You will also be touched and aroused emotionally—sometimes when you least expect it. You will become more aware of your body, and what your body can tell you. And you will be drawn to think anew about life's big questions: What is my life for? What gives my life meaning? What do I care about most? Does my life reflect my ideals? Is my life part of a greater whole?

Those big existential and spiritual questions are potentially as much part of your self-therapy as your immediate emotional concerns: how to listen, how to feel less angry, how to bear your loneliness, how to develop trust.

It is not a matter, either, of gradually progressing from emotional issues to existential and spiritual ones. With self-therapy, as with life, take it for granted that your exploration will be anything but linear! For all your increasing clarity and insight, there will be some situations when you feel confused, conflicted and miserable. But hot on the heels of those setbacks, and despite old habits of panic, there will be times of respite and even of transcendence, arising out of increased awareness, when all of life takes on a different and much brighter hue.

It is that openness to awareness I want to insist on, for we are not, I believe, the total of our experiences; rather, we are what we dare to make of those experiences.

A willingness to make something of your experiences, a willingness to be aware: that is all that you need for self-therapy to work for you—and a willingness to be changed, not by me, not by this book, but through increasingly close encounters with yourself.

Who needs therapy?

Do you need therapy?

Do you deserve the time that therapy takes?

Haven't you got more important people to think about than yourself?

Haven't you got more urgent things to do than contemplate your own navel?

Rather than answering those questions directly, I would like to share two anecdotes with you. Both arise from the heady, untypical period when this book's preceding 'mother volume', *Intimacy and Solitude*, was coming out.

I was ending a tour of my home country, New Zealand, to promote *Intimacy and Solitude*. I had spent five years writing that book, and five years preparing to write it, and while I knew that I had benefited from that period of sustained work, nevertheless I wanted the book to be part of a community of experience. So, I had approached the book's debut with a great deal of vulnerability, but now, on the last evening, I felt able to take in the audience's appreciation.

I was appearing at the Aotea Centre with feminist writer Lisa Alther, a long-time friend and one of the two women to whom *Intimacy and Solitude* is dedicated. The Aotea Centre is an important venue in the cultural life of Auckland. It was certainly affirming to be asked to speak there and nowhere could this have quite the poignancy as in one's homeland.

My prepared talk went as it should, and then it was time for questions. Several hundred people could see me, bathed in too-bright lights, but for me the audience was largely in darkness, my closest contact with them came through the sensed mood of the auditorium and the tone of individual voices. Some lively questions were put, and then a woman got up and said: 'I would like to know how much therapy you've had.'

This is a perfectly legitimate question to be asked of anyone who works with psychotherapeutic issues. What made me hesitate, baulk even, was that I was being put on the line in a country where, when I grew up, therapy was something weird and wickedly self-indulgent that happened in New York; a country where in some circles psychotherapy is still associated with madness and weakness, if not actual moral degeneration.

In that historical/social context, I was being asked in front of hundreds of people if I was not only the polished performer they had just seen speak but also someone who 'needed' therapy.

Without thinking too much about it, I replied, 'Well, as it's just the two of us here . . .' This New Zealand audience understood immediately the joke I was making and the point I was making along with it. Thankfully, they laughed. I moved from one foot to the other, leaned forward, and said, 'No, seriously, as we are quite alone in this room, let me tell you, I've had my share.'

The point I am making here is multi-layered. It involves acknowledging that second of hesitation *and* my belief that therapy is not shameful. What's more, having lots of therapy over many years is not shameful. And being interested in therapy and the questions therapy raises is not a signal that you can't cope. Nor is it a signal that, lost in self-issues, you have closed your eyes to urgent issues in the world outside yourself.

I believe that in its many forms psychotherapy is for the sick, the weak, the mad, the apolitical. I believe that psychotherapy is for the strong, the curious, the coping, the sane. (Many people are all those things some of the time.) Therapy can be—and has been for me—a lifesaver, literally the difference between psychic life and death. It can, less extremely, be a liberating means to open yourself up to the treasures as well as the pain of your inner world; a means to heal the past and live fully in the present. Therapy can also be a means to experience other people—in all their diversity—with new insights and appreciation. It can transform the way you understand social movements, historical processes, philosophical systems, literature, art, music, popular culture.

Therapy *can* lead to increased feelings of dependence, confusion and weakness, as it is often accused of doing. But it is more likely to lead away from such feelings towards a comfortable experience of deepened identity and pleasure in living.

My second anecdote is briefer, but connects with the first.

I was being filmed at my home in Sydney for a television interview, again about *Intimacy and Solitude*. At the end of the interview, the producer said, with a certain amount of reluctance in his voice, 'I really think I need to read your book.'

Without pausing to check my words, I replied, 'Imagine if you had been the person who needed to write it.'

My point here is that while I was speaking publicly—and authoritatively—about psychotherapeutic issues, I was also reminded that I can speak about them in part because of the sadness, madness and feelings of lostness which pushed me towards therapy to find other ways to live.

Indeed, the very experiences which any one of us would try to avoid have been, in my life, catalysts for discovery. Those unbearable times have—eventually—taken me forward at least as much as love, laughter and the satisfaction of good connections, and at least as much as the insight and grace which is there when we have the courage and will to seek it.

So, writing this book, I have not been separate from it. And indeed, in the way of these things, I found myself while working on it in the midst of a period of upheaval. Unexpectedly, urgently, I too needed self-therapy. Out of the urgency that accompanies pain and confusion, I was pushed to try afresh many of these ideas: because I needed to be sure they would 'work' for you, and because I too—all over again—wanted clarity and insight.

'Hope' is the thing with feathers—
That perches in the soul—
And sings the tune without the words—
And never stops—at all—

The wisdom self-therapy shares does not belong to me, nor to any single person. It has been mine as I have needed it, and will go on needing it. Now it is also yours. Yours to make your own; yours to hand on.

I've heard it in the chillest land—
And on the strangest Sea—
Yet, never, in Extremity,
It asked a crumb—of Me.

Emily Dickinson (254)

About self-therapy

Some of you will come to psychotherapy for the first time through this book. Some of you may be old therapy hands; others may currently be having psychotherapy of one kind or another, or be working as counsellors or psychotherapists. None of those situations precludes your working with these ideas. There is no ideal moment of readiness for self-therapy other than your wish to try it. Equally there is no limit to the amount of exploring you can usefully do—to understand your inner world more deeply; to make your life in the outer world more conscious and effective.

In writing this book, however, I have taken the most isolated situation as my guide. I have assumed that your self-therapy will be done alone and that you will have no one you can immediately share with. Many active meditations can be done alongside another person, but I have made it possible and useful to do them without a companion, and in ways that will be rewarding for the complete novice or veteran alike.

I have also taken it for granted that along with psychological issues, you will be interested in exploring the meaning-of-life questions that so often appear as psychological problems. Should you baulk at this, let me assure you that just as you do not need to believe in the power of your own imagination for your imagination to work on your behalf, so too you do not need to believe in God, a Higher Self, the collective unconscious or any other idea remotely connected with spirituality or mysticism in order to receive the guidance which will—inevitably—come when you learn to be still, to be open, and to listen. All you need is a fairly ordinary dose of curiosity and a willingness to accept that you *can* help yourself, and that in developing your intuition, creativity and respectful awareness of others, you will grow in self-trust and love.

In making this book of self-therapy available, I am offering an unambiguous statement that I believe self-therapy can support and empower an individual to live with heightened awareness and sense of choice. I am not suggesting that self-therapy sessions should echo or can replace individual psychotherapy or counselling when that is intelligently and respectfully done.

There is, for most of us, something irreplaceable about sharing experiences in the context of a relationship. However, the reality is that for many people there is no therapy available, good or bad. Costs, lack of facilities, a reluctance to disclose to someone else: these can all prevent someone from going into therapy. Also, for countless people, there is an urge to know more about themselves and others not matched by an urge to engage in a therapeutic relationship.

For those people, self-therapy has something specific and valid to offer, whether it replaces psychotherapy, precedes it or is done as an adjunct to it.

Self-therapy equally is not a substitute for the therapeutic qualities of satisfying interpersonal relationships. But in doing self-therapy, you enhance such contacts when they exist, and, when they do not exist, you increase your potential to find what they offer in less conventional ways.

Undertaking self-therapy does not lock you in to an arduous search for psychological perfection which only persistent training will reward.

Even intermittent use of *The Intimacy and Solitude Self-Therapy Book* will bring benefits. There is no set pace at which you must move, no warning that you will lose your 'mental health fitness' if you stay a month on a single active meditation, or keep this book on the shelf for a year before using it.

Using the *Self-Therapy Book* offers the pleasures of any voyage of discovery. It will challenge you. Sometimes you will want to avoid what you discover, but working through it ought not to feel like yet something else you must do to be a better person or to deserve love.

If you can make time for regular self-therapy sessions, you will build up a momentum that will in itself have a therapeutic value. But that may not happen immediately, and it will not happen at all if you are forcing yourself to do self-therapy because you are invested in an ideal outcome or are driven by a superego whose single command is 'should'.

Will self-therapy change my life?

The approach to self-therapy offered here resembles the kind of inner-self work many people are now adopting when they have a life-threatening illness.

Even the most conservative medical specialists recognise that work done 'on the inside' through meditation, visualisation and imagery exercises can sometimes prolong life when intervention 'from the outside' cannot. *It is important to acknowledge that you need not be faced with a terminal illness to gain exactly those benefits.*

Miraculous though some of those changes will be, I cannot, however, promise that self-therapy will bring you the experiences of intimacy that you long for, nor that periods of loneliness will immediately transform into positive experiences of solitude.

I make no guarantees about outcome: that might shut you off from possibilities you have not considered yet. What I can do is assure you that self-therapy will dramatically increase your capacity to see potential in formerly closed-off situations; that your knowledge of your inner world will grow like Jack's beanstalk, and as that changes, the outer world you know so well will be newly revealed to you. Who knows, you might even change your perceptions altogether about what you must have in order to be happy!

At a time when novelty and sensation are so valued in our societies, I also want to put in a plea that you approach self-therapy with modest expectations, thinking of it allowing gentle *shifts* of consciousness and behaviour, *shifts* in feeling and attitude. Such shifts, with time to assimilate them, would, over the course of even a single year, make for considerable gains of knowledge and empowerment.

I make this plea knowing that some of the exercises and meditations will immediately, even radically change the way you experience your inner world and, with that, the outer world of action and interaction with others. (For some of you, the discovery that you have an inner world, packed with images, memories and insights, will itself be transforming.) But there is a difference between changing your perceptions, attitudes and behaviours, and carving out a whole new 'you'.

Small, positive, personal changes; a greater sense of expansiveness: that's what I hope for, because as with *Intimacy and Solitude*, this *Self-Therapy Book* is not intended for self-development only. My goal in returning to this material is to intensify your awareness that when your inner world grows more real to you, so the outer world we all share becomes more precious, not just the tiny corner of it where you live, but all of it: the sky above and the earth below.

How to use the Self-Therapy Book

Please share my relief that it is impossible to use this book 'incorrectly'! Nor need you fear that you could damage yourself or do others harm by undertaking self-therapy using this book as your guide. Everything the *Self-Therapy Book* offers allies itself with your own instinctive urges towards psychological and physical good health. That means a healthy balance between self-love and self-knowledge, and awareness of, respect and love for others.

There is no set programme to follow and you need not move systematically through the book, but you will need to understand a few basic concepts: Meeting the Wise Being, visualising and finding images, using the Magic Wand, Free Writing and Free Drawing. Once you are familiar with those concepts—none of them difficult to learn—you can fly straight to a particular section or active meditation, ignoring the rest until such time as you need it.

Because this approach to self-therapy will develop your intuition (or trust in what you need), you may find yourself drawn to use the *Self-Therapy Book* at random, perhaps not knowing in advance why you are turning to an active meditation on anger, rather than continuing to draw and write about an aspect of gender as you had planned. Or you may decide in advance of your session to begin with a particular meditation, yet when you settle into your therapy space you realise that you want to do nothing but draw, or sleep.

Follow that intuition. From the sleep or time of reverie may come the dream you need to understand a worrying crisis. From the drawing may come an image which allows you to see the hidden side of a problem. Or perhaps you simply need a rest or to have a playful time with paper and crayons. That is also therapeutic.

When you want to stay with one thought or active meditation for some time, do so. *Repeating an active meditation inevitably deepens your experience of it.* There is no rush, no agenda. Tiny shifts in old habits, gently unfolding awareness: these are more likely to be woven into the fabric of your life, and to become your own, than dramatic resolutions or flamboyant new starts.

For some the index will be a secure way in, identifying a topic or feeling that seems urgent (grief, loneliness, self-blame, anger, separation) and tracking the different ways this book supports you in exploring it.

Readers can, of course, move systematically through the sections, trying all or most active meditations before establishing individual favourites. In organising the material I have been aware of those readers and have attempted to vary the shapes of the windows and doors and crevices that allow you to glimpse and experience new insights.

Knowing that some readers will be predominantly thinking people in whom a capacity for feeling needs developing, and that others may be awash with feelings yet find it hard to locate what they think in times of stress, I have mixed active meditations which draw on and release feelings with those where thinking is the predominant activity. While there are many serious discoveries to be made, there are also meditations to promote a sense of joy and creativity which can carry you through many a flat period or dark time.

The following guidelines will help you.

1 Set aside a regular time for your self-therapy You won't have magical results from every session. Some sessions will be obviously rewarding, others will feel like a waste of time. Those variations happen when you are seeing a therapist also. Oddly, some of the sessions when 'nothing is happening' or when you feel bored, distanced or irritable, precede a real breakthrough with whatever issue you are currently working on. (The boredom, the 'nothingness' is often part of your resistance to new information.)

Promise yourself that you will persist with your sessions, at least once a week, for three months. Without such a promise, it would be too easy to give up after a couple of nothing-is-happening sessions and miss the gems that could follow.

The time of day or night is not especially important. Privacy is, and confidence that you won't be interrupted. Take the phone off the hook. If there are other people in the house at the time, ask them to respect the fact that you are not available for any reason less than fire or flood.

2 When possible, have your therapy sessions in the same place
Build on the familiarity of that place, and its associations with the discoveries you will surely make. That too will help you through the flat times when only an act of will or faith will keep you going.

3 Have with you, always, the tools of your self-therapy trade
• Your journal (a large, blank-paged book with good quality paper).
• Paper for drawing and lots of crayons of the best quality you can buy (wax crayons are ideal).
• Pen and paper for writing (some people combine their writing, journal-writing and drawing into one big folder. That can work well to uncover patterns and links in your self-discoveries).
• A tape machine. Sometimes it helps to pre-record a guided meditation.
• Music—if that helps you to relax and is undistracting.
• Tissues. Sometimes you will feel upset, lonely or full of grief. You should not have to search for a tissue.

4 Work at your own pace   There is no hurry and no limit on the years you can spend in self-therapy. Gradually increasing awareness, an occasional deeply felt insight: that is enough for most people to bring into daily awareness. This contrasts dramatically with the Big Bang approach to therapy offered in large-scale workshops which promise to change your life. Such weekends are fine for an adrenalin rush, but their approach rarely has any lasting psychological effect. We are creatures of habit. *We like our habits*, even those that are doing us harm. Shedding habits which are not helpful to us (and they can be habits of feeling, thinking, acting or reacting) always takes time. It also takes confidence that what we are putting in their place is of value.

I have already urged a gentle, modest approach. Trust such an approach and the small steps that follow. Be grateful for them. One illuminating insight a week would add up to a fund of wisdom in a year—and a giant step into the life you want to be living.

5 Avoid talking too soon or too much about your self-therapy

Self-therapy is a time for your inner world. What you discover there will change the way you are in the outer world, and how people experience you. But when you are in the process of bringing into your conscious awareness hurts from the past, or working to integrate new insights in the present, it is rarely helpful to chat about them. Friends, with the best possible intentions, will tell you what they think! At the stage when your own discoveries are delicate and tentative, this will not help you. Equally, it is rarely helpful to show other people the drawings or the writing you do in your self-therapy sessions. Revel in your own restraint.

6 When you are in more pain than you can bear, get help

You will contact old wounds that make you feel sad, or even wild with rage, although you are unlikely to make discoveries that are more painful than you can tolerate. It helps if you know how vital it is to healing to uncover *what is there*, but that does not immediately stop the pain. If you feel in more pain than you can bear, *get help*. You are entitled to it. Most major cities have telephone crisis lines: they are a good place to start when searching out local resources.

Realising you need more help than self-therapy can give is not an admission of failure. Self-therapy can lead you into therapy with another person; it can support you as an adjunct to such therapy; it can exist entirely in its own right. Each experience is worthwhile.

Your individual self-therapy sessions

1 Re-reading Intimacy and Solitude   The *Self-Therapy Book* is written as an extension of the work I made available in *Intimacy and Solitude*. Except for occasional passages printed in bold type, I have not repeated here the theoretical insights which that book offers, but I do regard those insights as the essential foundation for this self-therapy. So, as you use the *Self-Therapy Book*, I would urge at least an occasional re-reading of the mirroring section in *Intimacy and Solitude* (Self, Women and Men, Intimacy, Solitude, Desire). This will concentrate your mind on those issues *and how they affect you*. It will remind you where your questions and uncertainties lie, as well as what changes you want, when change seems called for.

2 Time for your sessions   Your self-therapy sessions should last about an hour. You can have another session on a pressing issue the next day, should you choose, but extended sessions are rarely extra helpful. Equally, getting up after fifteen minutes or so, telling yourself that self-therapy is a waste of time, will create a self-fulfilling prophecy.

3 Getting started   Some people use music to relax. Others enjoy silence and a feeling of settling-in to this valuable time.

If you are following this book through its five sections you might spend some time reading the relevant section in *Intimacy and Solitude*, or re-reading just a paragraph or page or two and then allowing your thoughts to drift away from your outer concerns to what is happening inside you.

When I don't specifically draw your attention to what is happening in your body, move your awareness around your body, checking out what your body can tell you (see p 106). Keep your breathing deep and steady.

4 Using the active meditations   The active meditations are your focus for self-therapy. Even when an active meditation does not look as if it will take long, begin it fairly early in your session. Allow plenty of time for drifting with your thoughts, writing, drawing, expressing emotion, and jotting down your awareness of what is happening in the present, as well as what the active meditation brings up from the past.

5 Repeating active meditations When you repeat an active meditation, your associations will change and deepen. If you feel drawn to spend several sessions on a particular active meditation, then that is the right thing to do. They are a way in to your inner world, a bridge to very special discoveries. By repeating medita-tions you will also resist your own restless search for novelty and face the harder challenge of developing persistence and patience.

6 Be under-ambitious It would rarely be helpful to do more than one active meditation in any single session. If you run through the active meditation and wonder what to do next, draw or write freely. Or sit quietly, watching your thoughts (see p 41) until your hand again takes up the pen or crayon and your session continues.

Drifting, wasting time, staring out the window: these can all be part of your therapy, but if that feels too much like the rest of your life then focus your attention with a repetition of the same active meditation, or persistently writing out or drawing your reactions to what is happening in the present (see p 32), thus crashing through the habitual wall of your own boredom or avoidance.

7 Limit your urge to analyse Using your mind is essential to self-therapy. But you will also be working with the language of symbols—which is how your unconscious communicates with you. That means accepting you cannot always grasp intellectually or rationally what those messages mean. *There will be a meaning to discover, but not always in the way that you expect or that your mind wants.*

Use your therapy sessions to create balance between your mind and feelings, your rationality and intuition, your creativity and your urge to conform; to create balance between love and will. Develop those aspects of yourself which are less attended to or honoured in other areas of your life.

8 Ending a session Setting a time frame for your sessions, much as a therapist would do for you, frees you from worrying about whether you should stop now or later.

Take a few moments at the end of each session to slow your breathing, bring your awareness to your centre, and to look around the room, noting its familiarity.

If, as your session ends, you feel churned up, sad or angry, know you can have another session whenever you want. You may also want to turn to the brief Meditation on love (see p 221) or to awareness of your Wise Being (see p 23).

9 Be thankful A moment's thanks for any small moment of discovery or insight you have made during your sessions is surprisingly helpful. Who are you thanking? Your sense of that may vary according to your world view. Some people will be thanking God; others will thank themselves; others their Wise Being, the wisdom of the elders or the collective unconscious.

A moment's gratitude brings a moment's grace.

Such a moment can colour a day.

Your key self-therapy supports

The idea of self-therapy can seem lonely: sitting on your own with a book, coming face to face with your problems and pain with no one to hand you the tissues. Yet my experience is that no one is left lonely for long.

Self-therapy is connecting. It brings you into contact with parts of yourself you may have had little opportunity to know and it brings you more confidently and honestly into contact with others.

As valuably, it allows you to meet a 'therapist' who will be with you day or night, who will take no holidays, who will charge you no fees, who will never grow tired of you, and who will always regard you unequivocally as their favourite patient. This inner therapist—and the *Self-Therapy Book* guides you easily towards meeting him or her—is the Wise Old Man, the Wise Old Woman, or simply the Wise Being.

The Wise Being, as a symbol of the wisdom of your self, is at the heart of this approach to self-therapy. It is the source of discovering that, within you, is wisdom as great, as loving, as far-reaching as any source of 'knowing' you could find outside yourself.

It is always empowering to come into contact with the image or figure who personifies wisdom for you. What form this figure takes will be dictated by your own personal experiences and desires, as well as by the time and place in which you live.

A Wise Being is characterised by wisdom *and* by loving acceptance. A Wise Being who scolds, is malicious or who puts you down is decidedly not a Wise Being: it is a superego image which can be acknowledged and even named as a subpersonality (the Principal, the Prison Officer), but should not be confused with your source of loving wisdom.

Fifteen or more years ago, I did the guided meditation which follows for the first time and met my Wise Being. The figure who came to me in my opened-up imagination had already been with me in two or three memorable, life-changing dreams.

I was touched to see her again, and amused to notice how much she looked like the writer, Doris Lessing. (Our Wise Beings are bound by time and place!) She had grey hair swept into a bun, sharp or even rather fierce eyes, and a beautifully rounded, womanly body draped in a grey, soft tunic tied with a cord which I later thought looked much like a monk's robe or, more banally, like the clothes Alec Guinness wore to play Obi Ben Kenobe in *Star Wars*.

I used this Wise Being figure as inspiration for the court jester story in my novel, *Running Backwards Over Sand*. There she had the same robes, Lessing's piercing, embracing stare and maybe also the message that Alec Guinness delivered so powerfully to huge audiences in *Star Wars*: that 'the force' is with you. I would translate that to suggest the 'force' of wise love is *within* you, waiting to be drawn out and used—not for your own benefit only, also for the benefit of others.

As I have aged, my Wise Being has seemed more universal and, oddly enough, more 'herself'. But the aura of Doris Lessing the wise writer remains, perhaps because the wisdom that lay behind the writing of *The Golden Notebook*, a key book for me in my personal development, resonated with what I was most tentatively getting in touch with then in my own self, and personifying in my mind's eye. This wisdom I am talking about is not Doris Lessing's only, but she mediated it through her work in a way that most positively stirred me at a time when I was becoming conscious of a deeper, truer sense of self than had previously been available to me.

Such inner wisdom writers, artists, poets, musicians, thinkers, dreamers and mystics feel free to draw on. But it is not for them only. It is a wisdom that is available to any one of us, at all times.

Using the guided meditation which follows, you may feel that you are at once in close contact with someone/something you immediately recognise as your Wise Being, in much the same way you might recognise a beloved friend after years of separation.

But perhaps you will not have that experience for weeks or even months. Your relationship with your Wise Being might initially be cautious. It might demand from you a curiosity and tenacity which will take you back to this particular meditation again and again. You may not meet your Wise Being the first or even the tenth time you journey up the mountain. You will, nevertheless, make some precious discoveries each and every time you travel through the rich, unfolding landscape of your inner world.

Value those discoveries, be thankful for them, and remain confident that at the right time your Wise Being will become known to you.

Meeting your Wise Being

• Make yourself comfortable.

Be confident that you have time for a full self-therapy session without interruptions. You may want to record the meditation on a tape beforehand so that you can keep your eyes closed. If so, record it slowly, giving yourself ample time for relaxation and pleasure. You may have a friend willing to read it aloud, very slowly, and to be with you while you journey, without intruding. You may want to read the meditation through a few times and then simply remember it, telling it to yourself as you travel, and not worrying if you have done it exactly as suggested here.

Sitting comfortably, keeping your eyes closed, and shutting out the world around you so that you can enter the world within yourself: that's all that is needed.

• Take some time to be aware of where your back is resting, and of what is supporting you as you sit.

Enjoy the feeling of where your back and bottom and feet feel held and supported. Enjoy that support and sink into it. Open your hands, then feel them relax. Relax the muscles of your face. Relax the muscles of your tongue.

With your eyes still closed, roll your eyeballs towards the back of your head, and then slowly relax them forward in their normal position.

Be aware of the sounds around you. Know these sounds will fade as you move more deeply inside yourself.

Notice the breath coming in and out of your body. If you wish to do so, slow your breathing a little until it has a rhythm which is relaxed, easy, comforting.

If anything is distracting you, let it pass by. Watch it go. If it is something important it can be dealt with later. If you feel anxious, bring to your awareness that it is not possible to fail this meditation. Whatever it brings you, you can welcome.

• As you feel ready, imagine that you are sitting in a field or a meadow.

You may want to move your body a little as you experience with pleasure how clean the air feels in this lovely place; how green the grass is; how sweet the sounds of nature are—birds, insects, wind in the branches; how comfortable the grass is on which you are sitting. Perhaps the warmth of the sun is playing on your face. Your everyday cares will disappear now for a while. You can feel totally present in the moment.

Enjoy your moment for as long as you want.

• When you are ready to do so, and while continuing to sit comfortably with your eyes closed, you will see in your mind's eye that there is a path in front of you.

In your imagination, you will get up and walk on that path, feeling the ground beneath your feet, noticing how that feels. You will notice whether the path is well marked and easy to follow, or perhaps it is barely a track. Follow it, taking your time and enjoying the walk, enjoying looking around you, enjoying the reviving air and quiet and perhaps too your own sense of adventure as you realise the path is becoming steeper and is taking you upwards, towards a mountain.

• At the foothills of the mountain, there is a forest.

Pass through the forest, keeping to your path but noting what kind of forest it is, and how you feel as you pass through it. *Take your time*. Each stage of the journey has its own strengths and lessons.

When you do leave the forest, and continue to climb the mountain, be aware that you have the strength to make this journey. If at any point you need to sit and rest, you can do so. Continue with your journey when you are ready.

Notice the terrain you are passing through, in your imagination. Is the path well marked? Are you having to hold onto rocks for safety? Are there any creatures near you? Any flowers or trees you are particularly struck by or drawn to? Is there a rail when the path is narrow? Must you clamber and cling, or is it an easy climb? What sounds or smells are you aware of, if any?

• When you begin to tire, you will round the last bend. There, in front of you, is a plateau near to top of the mountain, bathed in warm light.

The feeling here is of great peace and love and forgiveness. Words can be used here, but are not necessary in this place.

This is your place. You can return to it at any time.

• When you are ready to do so, become aware that here, near the top of the mountain, is a most beautiful Temple of Silence. This Temple looks as simple, as beautiful, and as peaceful as you want it to be.

Inside, waiting for you, is your Wise Being.

The Wise Being may be a man or a woman, or their gender may be irrelevant.

• As you enter the Temple of Silence feel ready to see the Wise Being walking towards you, emanating a powerful feeling of loving acceptance.

Remember, the feeling you get in the presence of your Wise Being will be that of loving acceptance.

Should you not feel ready yet to see your Wise Being, know that you will do so at another time, and enjoy the beauty and healing peace of the Temple of Silence.

• If your Wise Being is with you, enjoy its presence.

You can ask your Wise Being for a word or a symbol (a visual image) to take down the mountain with you.

If you have a particular problem which you want to speak about to your Wise Being, formulate your request or question and state it clearly, knowing that the answer may not come right now, but only when you are ready to have it.

• As you enjoy the presence of your Wise Being, feel that quality of loving acceptance growing and expanding in you. Welcome it.

You can stay here, in this place, for as long as you want.

• When you feel ready to do so, say goodbye to your Wise Being.

Take with you whatever memories or images you have from the walk up the mountain, and this meeting. Those memories and images are yours. Enjoy them.

Take with you the confidence that you can return to this mountain and be with your Wise Being at any moment of your own choosing. That confidence is yours. Enjoy it.

• When you feel ready to do so, open your eyes, and bring your awareness slowly back into the present. Take some slow deep breaths, in, out; in, out.

• Take time to write about your experience in your journal, or to draw an image you received, or an image which arises out of the experience.

Here is a short account of meeting the Wise Being I wrote in my journal many years ago. I think it gives the flavour of discovery, and it may be consoling to anyone who does not have glorious experiences immediately.

'Finding the way up [the mountain] difficult at first. Briars. Pushing away the bush. Then the path becoming clearer. Enjoying the walk and the warmth of the sun and the feeling that the walk was within my control.

'The Temple is shining up there—open on all sides, white pillars, gold dome, very beautiful.

'As I got nearer I was walking on a mosaic path, very well cared for. Took off my shoes, stepped into the Temple. Beautiful, soft cushions everywhere.

'Stood in the centre and the sun fell on my hot body and I took that in.

'Then, through the same place that I was receiving the sun, my grey old woman from my dreams came, her clothes rather like a nun's habit, her hands outstretched like the Virgin Mary's.

'I felt so pleased to see her and that someone else would take control of things for a bit and I wanted to be small and to be held by her.

'When we were asked [by the person guiding the meditation] what we wanted to ask her I felt really confused, thought about several things and rejected them, then wondered about asking if I should get someone to live in my house.

'But the Wise Old Woman told me to be patient, what I want or need will come, to be patient.

'When we were told the Wise Old Being would give me a gift I felt she already had, but what she gave me additionally was trust. She said that she trusted me to find my way, to keep going somehow.'

Quick visits to the Wise Being

You can repeat the journey slowly up the mountain as often as you wish, taking a question or problem with you, but it is also possible simply to flash in on that wisdom and loving acceptance that your Wise Being symbolises by bringing to your mind the face of your Wise Being, holding that face steady in your mind's eye, and bringing your awareness of whatever is worrying or troubling you to the Wise Being.

If you are caught up in any unpleasant situation, or if you feel deeply disturbed or distressed by anything you are discovering through your self-therapy, you can freely summon the image of your Wise Being to comfort and guide you.

You won't always get an immediate answer, especially when you are asking for guidance around an issue laden with conflict. What you will get, however, is a crucial reminder that you can find answers within yourself.

If you return persistently to your Wise Being, the knowledge you are seeking might emerge in any of the following ways.

1 As an insight, or flash of clarity, while you are with your Wise Being or later.

2 Through a dream.

3 Through a feeling you must or should seek someone out to discuss your issue with them, or act in a way which is unusual for you. Perhaps this means being patient when you normally seek solutions—or being more active in asking other people for what you want or need.

4 Through your environment—for example, you may turn 'by chance' to a book and read what you have been needing to know or you may listen to the radio and hear someone speaking directly to your issue. Even a single phrase from a song or an overheard conversation may be all you are seeking.

5 Time itself may solve the issue for you, as events fall into place and you begin slowly to understand what pattern is unfolding.

The Magic Wand

The practice which follows is an adaptation of a technique used by Robert Desoille. He was a pioneer of the directed daydream technique of psychotherapy which echoes in both hypnotherapy and guided meditations. Its extreme simplicity to learn and use should not deceive you. It allows you to bring symbolic light to darkness and confusion. Once you have become familiar with the instructions below, you can use it quickly whenever you need 'light' to focus on a problem and see that problem from a fresh perspective.

You can also use the Magic Wand when you feel frightened or upset, and you can offer it as an empowering aid to children also. It is easy for most children to imagine, and can be a source of strength for the child who suffers from nightmares or fears of darkness, or lacks inner strength.

Sometimes when I am doing guided imagery work in workshops or with clients, and we need to go into dark, potentially frightening spaces together, I suggest they hold the Magic Wand. It always gives them the light they need.

You may want to record the following instructions on a tape.

• Take time to settle yourself comfortably. Close your eyes, reminding yourself that you are taking some valuable time away from your usual concerns and patterns of thinking. Slow your breathing; in, out; in, out.

• When you are ready to do so, ask your inner world for an image of a Magic Wand. As the image takes shape in your mind, look at the Wand, noting its details, its form, its length. Imagine holding it in your hand. Know how it feels. *Enjoy* having it in your hand. Appreciate its beauty, and the light it issues forth. Take all the time you need to recognise and appreciate your Wand.

Perhaps you don't have a particular problem you want to concentrate on today. If that's the case, just say goodbye to your Wand when you are ready, knowing that it is there to be used whenever you need it.

• If you do have a problem right now, and feel lost for insight, bring that problem to your mind. Focus on it for a few moments. It may be someone who is worrying you, a persistent troubling situation, or a feeling inside yourself you don't fully understand. If it is a feeling it can be helpful to see the word for that feeling written in your mind's eye.

• When you are steadily focused on what you want to understand, touch that problem—the word, person, situation or your image for the situation—with the Magic Wand. Hold your Magic Wand steady.

• Ask for illumination.

Sometimes you will see the troublesome someone or something, or a painful feeling, from a fresh perspective.

Sometimes *what lies behind the problem* will come to light.

Sometimes you will get an image of what you need, or need to be doing.

Sometimes nothing at all will happen right away.

• As you watch your Magic Wand, and the problem it is touching, repeat your request for illumination, but, as you do so, acknowledge your willingness to be patient, even playful. Accept that nothing may happen as you quite expect it, nor indeed quite when you expect it.

• When you are ready, let the image of your problem fade from your mind, along with the image of your Magic Wand. Remind yourself that you will get the insight you are searching for at the moment you are ready.

Here is an example of using the Magic Wand from Anna, a middle-aged, practical woman who often finds working with images difficult.

'I found myself wanting to draw a picture of a bear. This bear is coming again and again into my mind as I draw. I half believe that the same bear is menacing me in my dreams. Touching the bear with the Magic Wand, it metamorphoses into a man in a bear suit.

'I kept my mind focused. I was holding onto the Magic Wand all the time. And then as the light from the Wand intensified I was able to make out the features of the man. He turns out to be my father. I hadn't even been thinking about my father but I sensed at once that bear had led me to him . . . and to some thinking about him.'

Free Drawing

'A symbol is the best possible expression of something we have not yet understood.'

Peter O'Connor, *Dreams and the Search for Meaning*

Free Drawing is central to your self-therapy. The images that you put on the page are symbols for what you 'have not yet understood'. 'Thinking in pictures', as Freud put it, gives you direct access to your pre-verbal, forgotten past, as well as to conflicts and feelings in the present for which you may not have words.

You need have no 'talent' for drawing for Free Drawing to be useful. On the contrary, awareness of how you are drawing, and to a large extent what you are drawing, can be set aside.

Use white unlined paper and have to hand a generous supply of good quality, brightly coloured wax crayons.

• Find an image from within yourself. Follow your urge to put an image on the page—no matter how strange or inappropriate or 'difficult to draw' that image might seem to be.

• Allow your hand to move freely, following whatever image is emerging for you, without thinking too much about it.

• Allow yourself to feel led towards certain colours. Don't analyse or hesitate over your choices. Draw for as long as the energy holds, then stop.

• There is no 'correct' interpretation you must find when looking at your drawings, but in looking for clues consider what is happening in your life at present, and whether that brings up any association with the image on the page.

Treat all your drawings with respect. Don't feel that you must understand them at once. You may want to muse on an image for weeks before it reveals its message to you.

Eve was drawing bars, barbed wire, ugly fences—and all in dark slashes of black or brown. It took days of persistent drawing before she came to associate those drawings with a termination she had had a couple of months before, and her feelings about not having had a choice as to whether she could continue with that pregnancy.

It also possible to dialogue with the image: to set up a conversation in which you ask the fence, the fox, the heart what it wants or needs or is willing to tell you about your wants and needs ('Why have you come? Why have you come now?').

• It can help to speak or write as the image, using the first person ('I am an ugly fence, but I keep people out. I am strong and impenetrable. I am greasy and no one could climb over me . . .').

• When drawing seems impossible, and you face a blank page with a blank mind, pick up any colour at all and begin to move it across the page. This won't always produce an image you are happy with, but it will get you going. Quite quickly you will find you can approach Free Drawing with a sense of discovery.

In conventional terms I am hopeless at drawing, but in the course of preparing this book I rediscovered a drawing of two trees I did years ago which symbolised my relationship with Susanne Kahn-Ackermann, a much-loved friend. In the drawing the trunks of the trees and the leafless branches are separated increasingly, yet the roots are intricately entangled and grow from the same soil.

The meaning of this drawing may or may not have been clear to me at the time. I can't remember. But now, as Susanne lives in Germany and I in Australia, as I have children and she does not, as both of us are irregular correspondents, our branches and trunks— our life above the ground—are far apart, and sadly bereft of the leaves which might symbolise fresh contact. Yet our relationship continues to resonate in what we do, and what we do draws on the shared 'soil' of our past. Sexual politics, writing, publishing, therapy and, above all, spirituality, bind us together in the deepest core of our beings.

And that Free Drawing, done in a few moments, expressed it all.

Free Writing

Free Writing is not about 'quality' writing. It is about externalising internal thoughts and feelings, some of which may startle you. It allows you to discover *what you are waiting to know about your own self* and about issues that are closest to you.

When using Free Writing to explore an issue, the crucial word is, as with Free Drawing, 'free'. Don't stop to re-read what you have written, or to worry about your spelling or grammar. That is completely unimportant.

Sometimes you will write effortlessly, or your only problem will be writing fast enough to get everything down. There may be other times, however, when you need to return to your guiding sentence to keep going. This is the sentence which sets you off initially, and to which you can return repeatedly when you falter. Often I give a guiding sentence when I suggest Free Writing. If not, you can make one up of your own:

'When I think about giving up jealousy I . . .'

'Behind my anger is . . .'

'My life will be better when . . .'

In her inspiring book, *Wild Mind*, Natalie Goldberg suggests noting how you are feeling or what you are thinking and incorporating that into your Free Writing.

'I am finding this active meditation horrible. I feel sick and I want to stop and I would stop too but I said to myself I would write for ten minutes without stopping. It's the dog next door again. I would like to kill that dog for all the noise it makes when I'm so damned tired but the woman who owns it is pretty nice or at least I think she is because I never really have time to stop and talk to anyone . . .'

- Write for at least ten to fifteen minutes, without stopping, returning to your guiding sentence as often as you need to, even if you write virtually nothing but that sentence.
- Write persistently on the same issue and the crushing circularity and repetitiveness of your own thoughts will give way to the thoughts, insights and feelings crowding behind them.
- When you feel 'written out', read what you have written in the spirit of discovery, not of self-criticism.

Journal-keeping

Journal-keeping is an incomparable focus for discovery and exploration and an essential tool in developing awareness. It asks a certain level of commitment from you, but rewards that effort amply.

As with Free Writing, you will discover through your journal-keeping thoughts and feelings that are new to you, or only half guessed at. Seeing those thoughts written down makes them real. You can also take a step back from them in a way that cannot happen when they are part of a whirling kaleidoscope of mental activity. Taking that step back you can, gradually, begin to see patterns in much the same way your therapist would gradually distinguish patterns of thinking, feeling and attitude as you presented material to her.

It is your observation and gradual awareness of those patterns, habits, repetitions and associations that will allow you to be an effective self-therapist.

The 'talking cure' of psychoanalysis was achieved, Freud believed, by the analyst paying attention to the spoken word (and also to what is not spoken). Your self-therapy demands that you pay attention also: to what you 'speak' onto paper as well as to what you learn from images, and from the messages coming from your body.

You need not use writing only in your journal. Especially if you are a verbal person, it is helpful also to draw, putting onto the page whatever images arise from within yourself. Sometimes you may then feel moved to write, or simply to jot down a few words.

Journal-writing is part of many active meditations, bringing your self-therapy sessions into the everydayness of journal-keeping. More generally, journal-keeping will anchor insights from a self-therapy session and adds continuity to your self-therapy discoveries. (Reading my therapy journals from ten years ago, I can see how persistent some issues are, and note my progress on others.)

• Take whatever time is possible for you for regular journal-keeping, even if it is only ten minutes initially.

• Sitting quietly, with your journal open, let thoughts or images arise. Put them on the page, however trivial they seem. Don't feel that you must attend only to deep thoughts, or to sad or complex feelings.

• Write or draw as much or as little as feels right—but sit for your committed time, even if you are not constantly writing or drawing.

• Notice what you are thinking *and* feeling. Notice what is happening in your *body*. If you feel tense, note where the tension is. A shift in awareness and then posture may be all that's needed, but perhaps you find you want to flex your feet, shake or dance vigorously, lie in a bath scented with beautiful oils, or make a resolution to walk or rest more.

• Choose to notice what is positive in your life as well as what is problematic or painful. You could make it a habit to conclude your journal-keeping with a positive thought, or a quiet moment of thankfulness or affirmation. Often that mood will resonate long after the journal is closed.

Three of this book's active meditations especially enhance your experience of journal-keeping: Your inner happenings (see p 148), Finding the joy in your day (see p 149) and Reviewing your day (see p 255).

• At reasonably regular intervals, take an entire self-therapy session to read through your journal entries. This is the time to open your awareness to any patterns that are emerging.

Notice whether you need to strengthen your experience of love or will (your awareness of connections; your awareness of self-responsibility). Anchor your insights by writing them down.

Where there seems to be an urgent or painful issue emerging, resolve to give that issue the attention it needs.

Where there is cause for celebration, be lavish with your praise. You will not trivialise your therapy by having fun. You will enhance it.

'I notice I am less tense in general and much less tense at work.' HURRAH!

'Twice in the last month I have been able to listen to my children thoughtfully.' HIP HIP . . .!

'My list of hypothetical anxieties is shrinking.' TRIUMPH!

Even nothing has a shape

As effective as these techniques are (Meeting the Wise Being, Free Writing, Free Drawing, imaging or visualisation, the Magic Wand), I urge you to use them with an open mind and without the expectation of any particular outcome. Holding a desired outcome in your mind may prevent unexpected insights arising. Do please trust that at the best time, at the right pace, what you need to know will come.

It may be, however, that your urge to know is strong, or that you have had several painful sessions when nothing has happened as you have sat waiting for an image to arise in response to a particular issue or question.

Don't despair. Even nothing has a shape! When I am doing a guided meditation with a client and 'nothing' or 'I don't know' is all the information we are getting, it is possible to work with that.

I might ask any or several of these questions. You can use them too.

If you could give this particular nothing a shape, what shape would that be?

Does nothing have a colour? A smell?

If you could touch this nothing, and discover its texture, what would it feel like? Is it a rough nothing, a soft nothing, a hard nothing, a melting nothing, a tough nothing?

Is this particular nothing familiar to you? Does it remind you of anything or anyone? Does it remind you of a particular situation, or feeling?

If nothing could speak, what would it say?

What size is nothing? Is it a big or little nothing?

Is there anything hiding inside nothing?

Does nothing have a voice? What kind of voice is it? Would nothing be willing to use that voice, if not today, at some other time?

If you were to pay nothing no more attention, would nothing be relieved or disappointed?

Is there a small corner of nothing you can lift up, just to glimpse what is behind?

Does nothing have another name?

Is there anything that nothing needs?

Can you promise nothing that at some time you will be ready to see its shape, feel its feelings, speak to it and understand it?

• As you receive any information, no matter how tentative, jot it down or draw, or note a single word. For any information you get from 'nothing', be thankful. Nothing is a defence, there to protect you, perhaps long after such protection is still necessary. But move slowly, respectfully, and 'nothing' will inevitably transform into something.

PART ONE

Self: Exploring who I am

'Growth is understanding what we have not yet been able to conceive, feeling what we have never felt, doing what we have never done before. It is daring what we have never dared. It may not, therefore, necessarily be pleasurable. It obliges us to leave our comfort zone, to progress into the unknown, to face the tremendous impact of the Self.'

Piero Ferrucci, *What We May Be*

Introduction

Those people who have a sense of self have an inner reality, something virtually as precious as life itself because it markedly affects the ways in which you experience yourself and relate to others.

Growth, change, discovery, empowerment: these readily happen with your discovery of a deeper, wiser self than you can generally contact in everyday life.

In this section of the *Self-Therapy Book* you will discover ways to meet that wiser self and thus increase your awareness—your consciousness—about who you are and how you want to live.

—This will ease your dependence on how other people see and experience you as well as your dependence on what others need to provide.

—It will enhance your knowledge about what is happening in your life so you can know when this feels right for you.

—You will find you can be more 'yourself' in whatever situations of intimacy or solitude you find yourself.

You will experience this deepened sense of self in your own way, but here is Bettina's description. It reflects the experience of many other people also.

'I want above all else to feel alive in the world; to be able to be in contact with other people lovingly and respectfully yet without being walked over by them. In getting in touch with my core self I feel like I have become aware of something precious *that already belongs to me*. I realise I need not necessarily or always be overwhelmed by my daily concerns. That doesn't mean I am abandoning them. On the contrary, I'm now strong enough most of the time to cope with those daily concerns and yet still have energy left over for others.'

Discovering your sense of self

'The true Self is not an idea but an experience.'
Alan Watts

Discovering your sense of self is a lifetime process, not the goal of a single meditation. All the self-therapy you do will bring you more securely in touch with your own self, and inevitably closer to others. As crucial as this discovery is, the idea of self need not be approached solemnly. On the contrary, it is often best explored playfully and inquisitively.

• Relax your body and your mind. You are about to make an interesting discovery. Breathe in and out slowly, until you feel ready to think about who you are.

When you are ready, write 'I am . . .' followed by an aspect of your identity. Do this as many times as you can, reviewing different aspects of your life as you go.

I am a mother.
I am a daughter.
I am a shopping addict.
I am an environmentalist.
I am a computer operator . . .

• Now you have covered every angle of your current and past identity, imagine taking all those identities away. Strike them off your list, seeing them disappear as you do so. Mother . . . daughter . . . old girl . . . employee . . . choir member . . . keen shopper . . . secret reader of romances, etc, etc.

All those aspects of how people see and recognise you have been struck off. *Yet you exist*.

This is a step towards understanding the idea of self.

Watch your thoughts

This is a powerful active meditation and you will benefit from making it part of your daily routine, especially if you tend—as many of us do—to get caught up in your own thoughts, or even be overwhelmed by them. This beautiful little meditation can give you an exquisite, refreshing distance from those daily concerns, reminding you that you are
—more than your thoughts
—more than your feelings
—more than your attitudes
—more than your actions.

The meditation can take half an hour when that time is available to you, or less than five minutes when it's part of your routine.

• Take a few moments to slow down.

Sit comfortably, eyes closed. Breathe in, breathe out: slow and deep, slow and relaxed.

• As you sit, not expecting anything in particular, thoughts will come and go, some staying briefly, others for longer. *Watch your thoughts*. Don't push them away. Don't dwell on them.

• When you feel ready to do so, take a big breath—in, out—open your eyes, stretch. Be ready to continue your day.

But, as you go about your day, be aware that you were watching your thoughts. Who was watching your thoughts?

Your self.

Who am I?

Take your full self-therapy session for this active meditation which is adapted from Irvin D. Yalom's *Existential Psychotherapy*. You will need seven cards or pieces of paper and your journal for any comments you want to make. Before you begin, shake away any excess energy with a big, pleasurable shake of your entire body, then sit quietly for a few minutes, telling yourself you are going to take some time away from your usual daily concerns. Open your mind to what will follow.

• On each card, write an answer to the question: Who am I? Try to pose the question freshly each time to take you in to deeper layers of answering.

Who am I?

Write without censorship or judgement. Allow answers to arise from deep inside your being.

• When you have finished, take all the time you need to arrange the cards so that the answers closest to your core or deep experience of self are at the bottom ('I am an incarnated being with a purpose to my life.') and the more superficial answers, relating most to identity, are at the top ('I am an ardent golfer.').

• Study the top card. Ask yourself what it would be like to give up that aspect of who you are. Note your responses in your journal.

Move to the next card, and the next, until you have considered 'giving up' what is written on each of the seven cards.

Notice what emotions arise for you as you consider giving up an aspect or description of who you are.

Notice when it is a relief — or an impossibility — to consider giving up that expression or attribute of your self.

• When you have finished, allow some time to think and write about the experience you have just been through.

• Finally, integrate all those parts of yourself again by going slowly and respectfully through the procedure, but in reverse this time: starting with the core descriptions, moving (outwards?) to the less vital attributes of self.

• Later, when you write in your journal or return to this theme in your next session, you may want to

—Draw an image for what you feel, or something special you have discovered.

—Consciously appreciate a description or an aspect of yourself which surprised you or which needs honouring.

Reading your dreams

Your dreams can be an unparalleled source of information about the significant issues in your life. You do not need to be an expert to make good use of them.

Preparing yourself to take your dreams seriously means having to hand pen and paper so that you can scribble down your dream as soon as you wake or, better still, in the misty time when you are neither asleep nor awake. Write fast without analysing. Even a fragment is worth noting: a single image, a mood, an association.

I am often woken up prematurely by my dawn-loving children or our dog! Then whatever I was dreaming disappears before I can catch it. Despite this, the fragments I do gather build into patterns that give me information I could never have from waking moments alone.

In fact, collecting patterns and observing what is common to your dreams can be much less confronting than worrying about whether you have understood the symbolism or the hidden message of any single dream. Over time, you will see the same themes return. Or you may notice a mood or emotion consistently colours your dreams—and asks for attention. You may become aware that you are always in a crowd in your dreams, but are you part of the crowd or separate from it? How does that feel? Are you lonely? Are things very controlled in your dreams, or chaotic and disturbing? Do you have a companion in your dream to whom you can turn? Particular anxieties may persistently appear or perhaps in your dream you vividly express an aspect of yourself or a subpersonality which is not given much space in your conscious life.

• Before you go to sleep write the date on your page and any conflict or event that has marked that day. ('Saw a programme about Hitler. Carey got a bad report from school. I forgot to get vegetables and didn't have enough for dinner.')

• When you wake, write down as much of the dream as you can, writing in the present tense. ('I'm in a car and it's piled high with junk and we are speeding through a forest and my father is sitting on a rock beside the path and suddenly I can see we are headed for a waterfall and I know that I can't swim and I have no life jackets for the children . . .')

• If you wake with only a fragment ('I am heading for a waterfall.') or just a feeling ('I am frightened and don't know why.'), note that down.

• Observe any feelings that come up as you write down the dream. Notice which parts of the dream you find most interesting ('I love the slow-moving turtle.'). Jot down your associations ('I admired its unhurried pace when the car was going at top speed.').

• Feel confident about making your own associations to the people, creatures, objects or events in the dream. If you dream about an unexpected person, for example, ask yourself what attitudes, feelings or qualities you associate with that person. It could be generosity, bad temper, a sense of adventure—or any one of your vast reserve of emotions and attitudes that are represented or personified in your dream by an individual, creature or object.

• Freely dialogue with a person in the dream, or with a creature or object. If the dream is upsetting or disturbing, this dialogue can be especially helpful.

'What does it mean that you are present in my dream?'

'What do you want to tell me?'

'What do I need to know at this time?'

When you feel frustrated because the dream seemed to stop too soon, ask the person or creature what was going to happen next. Writing down whatever answer you get can help to anchor the dialogue and give you something solid to look back on.

It is also possible to use Free Drawing (see p 30) as a way in to a deeper understanding of a puzzling dream. Draw a feeling, a scene, talking to it as you do so. More information will emerge.

Here is how Christa worked on a dream in her first guided session. She had already written down her dream in the present tense.

'I'm walking towards a house. It's apparently very pleasant. I go in and walk through it. I walk a long way until I am standing on a balcony looking out over the ocean. The house is now much more dilapidated. It is owned by two gay men and the front part is very chic. The balcony is precarious. I dive from the balcony and swim under water for a long way. Then I realise I must swim back again under water. This time I am aware that Anthony [her infant son] is with me and I am very anxious as I don't think he can hold his breath for long enough under water. Andrew [a friend who is adventurous and can swim well] offers to dive with Anthony on his back as he can swim quickly. I feel that I must ask Redmond [Christa's rather possessive husband] and to my surprise he agrees. I am pleased. They go off. How do I get back? I don't know.'

Christa's associations with the 'characters':

Andrew: brave, physically confident, able to cope with danger.

Anthony: vulnerable, anxious, easily dead.

Redmond: dangerous, can't save me; unexpectedly permissive and kind.

The gay men who own the house: stylish, their things look good, but as the house extends towards the water they have less and less to do with it, and the house is more chaotic as it is affected by family life and men–women themes.

Christa's associations with the setting:

Things are not always what they seem. The house goes on much further or deeper than it should. Initial appearances can't save me. When it comes to my relationships with the two heterosexual men and my own son I am in deep water—out of my depth.

Christa's associations with the dream's themes:

Wanting to save Anthony. Unable to do it by myself. Too weak and timid. Knowledge in the wrong areas (above water, not below). I am a danger to my child. Took him into a dangerous place because I wanted to dive. I can't get or give enough nourishment. Redmond is my jailer. Andrew represents a freedom I can't have. Redmond can't have it either but he can give or withhold permission. I need to explore further how I feel about that.

When Christa is more experienced, she may come to see those characters a little differently and a little closer to home. She may, for example, come to recognise the infant Anthony of her dream as a pointer to her own child-self who feels terribly vulnerable and in need of protection from the Eternal Mother (see p 120). She might understand that her uneasy collusion with real-life Redmond's efforts to restrict her is an external expression of her own inner restrictions, and that the bold Andrew in her dream is part of her own animus or masculine side which has the potential to be more adventurous than she believes is possible for her at this time.

What Christa needs to gain those insights is nothing more than a lively, open-minded curiosity and a willingness to be patient when making her own individual associations with elements within a single dream, and with patterns that will emerge when she looks at her dreams cumulatively.

Living with the Rose

'The realization of the Self, the inner center, corresponds to the opening of the flower brought about by the vivifying action of the sun, the symbol of the spirit.'

Roberto Assagioli

'Living with the Rose' can be a reviving part of your daily life. It is a psychosynthesis exercise, created originally by Assagioli and included by Piero Ferrucci in *What We May Be*. My version is slightly adapted and can be done slowly and thoughtfully when you have time, and much more rapidly when you need to remind yourself, in the midst of your busy routines, that you do have a life beyond what is keeping you distracted and maybe drained.

You may want to tape the meditation before you use it the first few times. Allow plenty of time for pauses and, before you begin, remind yourself that if the image which emerges is startling or even distressing, this does not mean you have done the meditation incorrectly. Nor does it mean that your inner world is a disgusting place. The images that come in guided meditations, as in dreams, may take some time to understand and are most easily understood in the context of what is happening in your everyday life.

Drawing your associations with a particular image, or writing down words associated with the image, can help you receive its message. 'Worrying at it' is rarely helpful. Keep your mind open to what the image is saying, whether the image is immediately welcome or is taking longer to accept.

• Calm your mind.

Relax your shoulders, neck, head, throat, eyes, tongue. Relax your arms and hands. Welcome these next few, quiet moments.

• When you feel ready, imagine a rosebush. See in your mind's eye its roots, branches, leaves. On top is a rosebud. The rosebud is closed, enveloped by green sepals.

• Now see the sepals begin to open. Slowly they roll back and as they do so the petals inside are revealed to you. They are tender, delicate, still closed.

• Now the petals themselves begin to open. As they open, you will find yourself becoming aware of a blossoming which is also occurring in the depths of your own being.

Something in you is opening and coming to light in a way which is appropriate to your life in the present.

• As you continue to visualise the rose, you feel that its rhythm is your rhythm, its opening is your opening. You keep watching the rose as it opens up to the light and the air, as it reveals itself in all its beauty.

• You smell its perfume and absorb it into your being. You smell it with delight.

• Now, gaze into the centre of the rose, where its life is most intense. Allow an image to emerge from there. This image will represent what is most beautiful, most meaningful, most creative that wants to come to light in your life right now. It can be an image of anything. Just allow it to emerge without forcing it or holding onto any particular expectation.

• Stay with this image for some time. Absorb its quality fully.

The image may have a message for you. Allow yourself to be receptive to it. Perhaps the image itself is all the message you need.

• When you are ready to do so, open your eyes and take time to bring yourself back into your familiar surroundings. Take time to think about what you have experienced and draw or write if that seems appropriate.

After writing out the instructions for this irresistibly lovely exercise, I closed my eyes, moved through the stages of the rose coming into bloom, and out of the rose stepped a Sugar Plum Fairy, a tiny creature with a star on her head and a wand in her hand who looked exquisite—and very naughty!

I have little idea what this means yet, beyond a charming aura of playfulness, but I will return to enjoy the image until I feel its meaning is revealed to me. After all, the image arose from within me, *and so can its meaning*. It is useful to remember that with any dialogue with symbols, I am expanding my awareness of what is happening in the present, not surviving a test of my symbolic skills. But a fairy . . .?!

Self-expressions

With my acts, I express myself.

With my words, I express myself.

With my thoughts, I express myself.

With my gestures, I express myself.

With my habits, I express myself.

In the way I work, I express myself.

With my relationships, I express myself.

With my body, I express myself.

With my sexuality, I express myself.

With my life choices, I express myself.

Through my attitudes to others, I express myself.

This active meditation is not unlike the old idea of examining your conscience. Whatever your resistances to that notion, it can help clarify where you are not yet expressing yourself as truthfully as you might. Equally, it allows you to appreciate where you are being real in your expression of self. It is often thought-provoking —even challenging—and may occupy you over several self-therapy sessions.

• Think about each line *individually*, allowing images of yourself and your actions, words or thoughts (and so on) to move in front of your mind's eye. See yourself as others might see you (from the outside), then as you see yourself (from the inside).

• Write down all your associations to the line you are reflecting on. Don't censor what you write. Write; withdraw and reflect; write, reflect; write, reflect.

• When you have explored the line fully—for at least fifteen minutes—re-read what you have written. Who are you trying to please? Are there other ways to behave that would feel truer to who you are, yet are still sensitive to what others want?

• Before you finish with any one reflection, check if there is any modest change you want to make. Note it in your journal so you can monitor and support that change. Choose whatever quality you need to support the change (see p 145).

Discovering your self through drawing

Over a slow, leisurely series of self-therapy sessions, use images to explore various aspects of your experience of self.

I encourage clients to draw often in both group situations and individual work. They—and I—find it helpful 'beyond words'. Perhaps after doing this particular series of drawings you will be encouraged to sit quietly and ask your inner world for an illuminating image whenever you feel confused or disturbed. Drawing the image out, talking and listening to it, can frequently give you deeper insight than worrying or rationalising ever could.

You can extend this method of drawing single or paired images to explore your self in relation to work, your parenting, sexuality, spiritual concerns, political work, your vision for your life. You can also use it as a way to 'draw out' your understanding of a dream, or persistent anxiety.

Before you begin each session, take time to settle yourself comfortably. Remind yourself you are about to take some well-deserved time away from your usual concerns to explore your inner world in a creative, open-minded way.

Choose which image you are interested in exploring during the forthcoming session. Hold that focus in your mind ('An image for my child-self'). Sit quietly, body relaxed, until an image arises. The image may be delightful, but it could be unpleasant or even frightening. No matter what its mood, take time to draw it, and then at least as much time to listen quietly to your inner voice as you ask the image what it wants to tell you and why it has come to you at this particular time.

When no image arises, ask yourself what this particular 'nothing' looks like, feels like; what it reminds you of. Is it a big nothing or a little nothing; squeezed tight or buoyant? Is something hiding in the space you are calling 'nothing'? Perhaps 'nothing' has a colour. Start with that colour.

As you look at your drawing, observe what colours you used (or didn't use); how much space your drawing occupies on the page; the close or distant relationship between images; the 'tone' of what you drew. Observe how your drawing 'speaks' to you through the language of symbols, 'saying' what cannot easily be put into words.

After each session, note in your journal what you became aware of while drawing; what insights you gained—if any; what still mystifies you; how you feel now as you look at the drawings, and any small resolution you may want to make.

Each one of these efforts will be enough for a single session.

There is no limit to subject matter, but the five aspects listed below are a helpful way to start.

1 **Draw an image for your inner self** Then, go back inside yourself and find, and then draw, an image for the self the world sees.

Put them side by side, or draw them on a single sheet of paper. If the two images differ, discover (by asking each one of them) if they have something to say to each other. Do they want to give you another image that will help them come closer together? Is there any other help they want from you at this time?

Ask your questions, and just wait quietly, with an open mind, to see what answers come. Jot down any thoughts or feelings that arise.

2 Draw an image for your childhood experience of self Does that child-self image need something from adult-you: attention, will, understanding, love? Can you supply that? (The active meditation on p 120 will help.) If your child-self is in pain, does your Wise Being (see p 23) have a healing image to offer? Does your adult-self need to be reminded of anything worthwhile you left behind in childhood (how to have fun, be spontaneous, open to other people)?

3 Draw an image for the way you feel about yourself This image should arise from within to express how you feel about yourself in a particular, maybe troubling relationship (an image of yourself as lover, as daughter, as mother, father, colleague).

Now draw an image *for the self of the other person* involved in that relationship. Take your time, with eyes closed, to meditate on the idea of the other person as a self (see p 159) until an image arises which expresses that for this moment.

Allow the two images to speak and listen to each other by asking each of them what they need, want to say, how they could be helped or better understood.

As you look at the two drawings together, do they tell you anything fresh about this relationship?

Are there any issues you need to explore further, or changes you need to make?

4 Draw an image for your environment Environment here could be your home, your workplace, the city in which you live, your country, the planet.

Draw an image that expresses how you feel, as a self, in relation to that environment.

Allow those two images to speak and listen to each other.

Could you be giving anything extra to your environment?

Is there something important you need that you are not getting from your environment? How could that change?

5 Is there an image or word that describes what your self is longing for? Take time with this. Write or draw whatever comes to mind, then formulate a simple resolution in your journal to attend to what you have discovered.

Holding onto positive experiences

A very young child can only believe in what is present. When the mother of a toddler goes out of the room and the child screams . . . he may be screaming out of an uncomprehending fear that the mother who is disappearing is disappearing forever and, worse yet, that she is taking with her their shared sense that he is Someone. Without her presence assuring him that he is Someone, he may be No one. This threatens total oblivion.

Here are two important questions to consider. They may be difficult at first to grasp, but are worth the effort.

Can you take in and hold onto positive experiences, even when the experience is over?

Can you retain positive experiences of other people, even when they are not with you?

In exploring these sensitive questions, your mind can be your ally.

• Choose a recent positive experience, however minor. Replay it slowly in your mind, freezing it every few seconds and saying to yourself: *That good experience happened to me.*

• When you have taken all you can from the memory, spend some quiet moments enjoying the feeling of having taken in something nourishing, and having kept it alive inside you.

• Notice whether it is difficult for you to do this and whether discouraging or self-denigrating thoughts fight for space in your mind. Use this experience to explore what your usual thought patterns are when something good happens. Do you dismiss it? Downplay it? Do you feel uncomfortable or unworthy recalling positive events or interactions? Do you question whether you deserve happiness, praise or positive experiences?

Such negative habits of thinking can be changed.

• Return to your memory of the positive event.

Bring to mind a word or an image which conjures up that event for you.

• Draw that image, or write down the word—big and bold.

This will give you something tangible to hold onto when you feel the positive experience slipping away, and feelings of uncertainty taking its place.

This image might arise from the event itself. Equally, it could be a golden net, a vase, or any container in which your positive feelings can be safely cherished, increasing your capacity for self-love and self-acceptance.

As your capacity to hold good experiences increases, you will find it easier to hold onto positive experiences of people also, even when they are not with you; even when they seem to be choosing not to be with you.

• Don't let good times slip away. Recall them in your journal. Anchor them with an image or a word. Be thankful for them.

When the voice of your self-denigration mocks you and belittles those events or your warm memories, simply tell yourself that the voice is protecting old habits. Let the voice be heard, then let it fade. Remember: *the positive experience lives in you.*

Colour, culture, gender, class

In the way you experience self, and the selfhood of others, you will express your attitudes towards colour, culture, gender, class.

Here is Evelyn speaking. Her mother is white. Her father was black.

'He was a clever man and good at anything he did. But no matter how good he was at his job he was never the boss, never top. Coloureds, he used to say, can never be better than second.'

Here is Sean speaking, a man who grew up in a conventional family in a wealthy suburb.

'I thought everyone had swimming pools. I am ashamed of my ignorance now but I thought poor people had smaller pools and only one car.'

Here is Sandra speaking, an Englishwoman married to a Spaniard.

'The great thing about learning to speak Spanish and to be a Spanish wife is that when I open my mouth and talk I am appreciated for my efforts as a foreigner speaking Spanish. I am not judged and categorised immediately because I have a lower-middle-class, provincial accent.'

In exploring this issue, it will help to recall an actual situation when your preconceived ideas about others were challenged. Perhaps it was at work, in a public place, at a party, or when a story in the paper or on television jolted you to confront your own fixed patterns of thought or attitude.

• Re-run that situation now, intensifying your awareness of when your outlook is limited by strongly held opinions or prejudices. (Women can . . . Gay men always . . . Asians never . . . Black people are . . . White people wish . . . Working-class people can't . . .)

Jot down your thoughts or insights in your journal.

• Allow that particular experience—and any others that come to mind—to tell you how your opinions and prejudices could affect the ways in which *others see you*.

Is this the way you want to be seen? Does it accord with who you are? Is there any way you could signal a more open, respectful attitude that encompasses difference as well as similarity?

Again, write down your thoughts as they occur.

• Now visualise yourself meeting each person and situation with an open mind free of preconceptions. Check out how that feels: in your body, your breathing, your physical stance, as well as in your emotions and your thinking.

• Take time to note in your journal any shift in attitude or behaviour you want to make. *A shift in feelings will follow*.

Promise yourself to review this important issue regularly.

Beyond the obvious

With any exploration you make of self/other issues, it is worth asking yourself if you are echoing stereotypical attitudes that are part of your socialisation. If so, how can you bring to each person you meet the qualities of a self-with-self encounter?

• When you feel unable to set aside your prejudices about a particular individual's age, size, sexuality, colour or gender—or political or religious beliefs—it is worth taking time to meditate on the self of the other person. That may give you a sense of the person beyond the body that clothes her or him, or even beyond the attitudes the two of you carry into your encounters. Meditating on the self of another person is explained on p 159.

• It is also very helpful to imagine what it is like to be that person. One way to try this is by writing a letter to yourself, *as though it were from that other person*.

This is how Gina did it. She has an Indian boss and Gina found she was facing her own racism in her resistances to being told what to do by Meera.

'I spent time thinking about Meera, getting myself mentally into her clothes, her body, recalling her facial expressions and the way she moves. When I felt I'd captured that and had lost some of my self-consciousness, I began to write, "Dear Gina . . .", all the while thinking my way further into Meera's head.

'It didn't work one hundred per cent. There were definitely times when I was writing as Gina and not as Meera, but at least some of the time I did feel connected to Meera's pride and anxiety, and what I was left with was a better sense of how she feels as an Indian woman in a predominantly white office where people are competitive and judgemental, and also her common-or-garden anxieties about being a woman in a position of authority and how she wants that authority, but it's hard for her and so she sometimes uses it awkwardly.

'After that I could feel more empathy and while we haven't got to be friends, I do feel we are getting along well enough and I can say what I feel more truthfully and without guilt that racism is firing my remarks.'

Living three lives

D. W. Winnicott, English psychoanalyst and wise theoretician, has suggested we need three simultaneous lives.

1 A life in the world with interpersonal relationships as 'the key even to making use of the non-human environment'.

2 A personal, inner reality. 'This is where one person is richer than another, and deeper, and more interesting when creative. It includes dreams (or what dream material springs out of).'

3 A life of cultural experience. '[This] starts as play, and leads on to the whole area of [human] inheritance, including the arts, the myths of history, the slow march of philosophical thought and the mysteries of mathematics, of group management and of religion.'

Winnicott suggests that of the three lives, this last is the most variable.

Exploring these three lives can be done to good effect in the company of a trusted friend. This is a rich and surprisingly provocative exploration.

• Allow yourself time to muse on the meaning of each of those three lives—and their interconnectedness—for you. Jot down any early thoughts you may have, or even single-word associations.

• Consider how circumstances or inclinations have led you to develop one aspect of your life more than the others. Which of those three areas was privileged in your family of origin; which ignored; which denigrated?

I am aware as I write that people can lead a highly developed 'cultural' life, but do so as spectators, without relating this in any meaningful way to their own inner explorations, or to the way in which they conduct themselves in their interpersonal relationships. Cultural activities may feed their senses, or their longing for novelty, but do not shift their experience of self and others. I guess political art is all about resisting, subverting, provoking in the face of such tenacious passivity.

• Use as many as seven cards to explore further each one of the three lives (the extrovert, introvert and cultural-expressive aspects of yourself).

On each card write your thoughts and reactions to the life you are exploring. Stay with one life—writing, withdrawing into yourself with eyes closed and mind relaxed; writing, withdrawing —until you have delved beyond what you most obviously know.

When you have finished, spread all the cards on the floor. (You may have as many as twenty-one.) Get a sense for the breadth and depth of those three lives; the points at which they intersect or seem at odds. Where are there gaps? How do you feel about those gaps? Are there over-fed or starving areas? Are those areas you need to acknowledge and begin to accept or improve?

Write down your insights and reactions as they occur.

• Choose to make a small shift in emphasis towards whichever aspect of your life needs conscious support and attention.

Take time to decide how you might do that. Use your Magic Wand (see p 28) if you need to, or ask your Wise Being (see p 23) for inspiration.

Note any resolution you make in your journal.

A single word on a decorated card may bring you the energy and inspiration you need to carry the change through (see p 145).

• Celebrate self-therapy's support of your 'second' and 'third' lives: your inner, personal reality as well as your creativity.

Creative living

Creativity strengthens your feeling of being alive, of being yourself. You don't need any exceptional talent to live creatively; it is simply *your personal reflection of aliveness*. All your self-therapy supports you in living creatively, but here is a meditation which focuses on it specifically.

• Approach the following list playfully! You may want to write it out, sing it aloud, stomp it out like a rap poem. However you approach it, let it get some rusty wheels turning. Add to it freely. Put on a portable card any sentence or idea which especially inspires you.

When you surprise yourself, you are being creative.

When you can look at something outside yourself and experience its unique reality, you are being creative.

When you can see a challenge and are prepared to *adapt yourself in order to meet it*, you are being creative.

When your imagination ticks as you do boring work, you are being creative.

When you shift your awareness from what is frustrating you (waiting for a bus) to what is all around you (human life) you are being creative.

When you are ready to absorb new information and allow it to change you, you are being creative.

When you approach a familiar person *as though for the first time*, you are being creative.

When you approach a familiar task *as though for the first time*, you are being creative.

When you can experience adversity as a challenge, you are being creative.

When your hand holds a pen or crayon and produces a reflection from your own imagination, you are being creative.

When you can identify with someone else's experience and add it to your own, you are being creative.

• Between this self-therapy session and the next, take time to appreciate your own creativity.

Decide how and where you can extend your creative (personal and alive) impulses and responses.

• Create a creativity chart for your wall, extending your list of possibilities (as creatively!) as you wish.

Use coloured papers to add new thoughts. Stick words or pictures onto your chart, collage-style. Does it look messy—or artistic? That's beside the point! The chart's function is to remind you how alive you can feel when reacting freely, and appreciating all that is exciting and possible even in the most apparently mundane of lives.

Respecting the creativity of others

'That's not the way to do it. Do it this way.'

Has there been an occasion in the last week or month when you have interrupted someone else's creative (personal) experience, to push them to behave, react or act in your way—rather than their own? This can so easily happen between parents and children, or teachers and children, and it can also happen between partners in a close relationship, especially when one person feels somewhat martyred or downtrodden.

• Relax your body and mind. Open yourself up to your own

imaginative and creative powers. Now recall that situation when you interrupted, corrected, derided, misunderstood or somehow spoiled another person's pleasure.

Go through it in some detail, looking at it from the outside as though everyone involved—including yourself—is an actor in a film you're observing. As you see the scenario unfolding, notice what you were feeling, what justifications sprang to mind, what mixed messages you were tussling with. Observe your tone of voice, your breathing and your body language.

When you have re-run the scene from start to finish, note in your journal what you observed. Take at least fifteen minutes for musing and writing. Be especially attentive to your habitual self-justifications. These might point you to an area of life you need to care for in a more positive way.

('It was the mess I couldn't stand. I knew they were having fun but it just felt like more mess to me and no one ever clears up the mess except me. My voice was shrill and hateful, and I was gripping the back of the chair with all my strength.')

• Now run that scene through in your mind again but this time visualise how it would be simply to allow the other person to have their experiences *in their own way*.

See yourself holding back. See yourself choosing to remain silent. See yourself shifting your attention away. Notice how that feels in your body, how you are breathing and with what difficulty you are resisting old habits of intervention.

Write about those feelings—including your bodily reactions—in your journal. Again, take at least fifteen minutes to write and think.

• If you can already anticipate how difficult it will be to restrain yourself from interrupting, devise and practise a simple strategy. This might involve aware breathing ('Breathing in I calm my body; breathing out I smile'). Perhaps you can imagine throwing over your shoulders a shawl of magical patience. (Notice how good it feels to have the shawl on your shoulders.) It might be that your children's/partner's/colleagues' activities are the permission you need to retreat to a chosen activity of your own.

• Between this self-therapy session and the next, try bringing your creative awareness to *the loving act of standing back*.

Continue to monitor your progress in your journal, reminding yourself that when your needs for play and creative expression are also met, you will be much less critical or envious of others in their play, their creativity—even their mess.

You deserve time to play.

Choose a symbol for this moment

This moment in your life emerges from all other moments to this point. Perhaps a symbol can best express your life right now. Symbols chosen by others have been as various as bread, an autumn leaf, a stone, a mountain, a shell, a balloon, a rosebud, a ball of fire. There are no limits.

• Take time to settle comfortably, slow your breathing down and turn inwards. Relax your body, letting tension go.

• Now ask your inner world for a symbol for your life in the present. Take time to let a single image emerge. If nothing happens, stay relaxed! You have planted a seed, a request, in your mind. Something will come when the moment is right. Now simply enjoy the calm, quiet space of waiting, drifting, dreaming.

• When you have chosen a symbol—or when a symbol has chosen you—explore its meaning by speaking or writing as that symbol: ('I am smooth on all sides, heavy, dark grey with unexpected speckles . . .').

• You can also talk to the symbol, listening quietly for the inner voice or image that responds to your questions.

'Is there anything I need to be doing differently at this moment?'

'Where can I turn for help around this problem?'

'How should I be with my partner in her pain?'

'When I look at your dried-up appearance and curling edges I feel sad and drained. How can I refresh you?'

As with all symbol work, an answer may not be immediate. It may emerge hours or days later: through a dream, a conversation, a 'chance' insight.

If the symbol is unpleasant or distressing, try not to judge it too harshly, but continue to talk to it. 'Why have you chosen to come? What are you wanting to tell me? Is there anything you need? Is there anything I need to understand? Can I help you reveal your hidden meaning to me?'

It is always possible to take a symbol to your Wise Being and ask for guidance (see p 23) or to use your Magic Wand (see p 28).

Borrowing the behaviour you need

'If one is to love oneself, one must behave in ways that one can admire.'

Irvin D. Yalom, *Existential Psychotherapy*

You *can* bring about immediate change in your behaviour. The potential for any behaviour lies within you and only needs your awareness and will to bring it out. Once you have used the following technique a few times, you can virtually switch behaviours mid-event when you are aware that old patterns are letting you down. Here is the way I suggest learning it.

• Review a recent situation when your reactions or behaviour felt unproductive of your own or others' wellbeing. Without wallowing in shame, be clear what you did not admire.

• Now choose how you would like to behave in that situation.

Identify what quality is needed as a foundation for that desired behaviour (patience, open-mindedness, resourcefulness, flexibility, modesty).

You are entitled to that behaviour.

• Close your eyes, withdraw into yourself. You are calling on your creativity to be your ally.

See yourself opening a big closet in which all positive behaviours hang. Each one has a clear label. Go to the behaviour you want. Take it for yourself. It will fit you perfectly.

Now you are 'wearing' that desired behaviour. Re-run the difficult situation in your mind, this time seeing yourself acting, reacting and behaving in ways you can admire. Note your feelings in your journal, as well as any resistances.

• Be conscious of who you are trying to please—or impress—with these changes. A positive change in behaviour will affect your feelings of self-love and the way that others experience you; but the goal here is not to deceive others, or gain advantage, it is to be true to yourself.

Anchor the experience with a reminder that you can return to that closet whenever you need to.

Here is how Benny used this exceptionally effective active meditation.

'I usually feel worn out when I get home and am impatient and ratty for the first hour or so until I wind down. By then everyone's pissed off with me, so I decided to do it differently. I practised it a few times in my mind first: I saw myself walking into the house and greeting everyone lovingly and *behaving as though* I wasn't tired and was delighted to see them.

'It worked, and I got a lovely response from the family.

'Sometimes I forget or I'm flooded with self-hate or self-pity or I'm too tired, but then I go through the rehearsals again in my mind: borrowing the behaviour I need to get through that first rough hour. It's dynamite.'

A laughing self

'Humor's most important psychological function is to jolt us out of our habitual frame of mind and promote new perspectives . . . We must learn to give fun a high priority in life. Like all other positive change, this also develops from the first essential step—learning to love ourselves.'

Bernie S. Siegel, *Love, Medicine and Miracles*

Leading a serious, 'meaningful' life, it is only too easy to neglect laughter—or even the capacity and willingness to smile.

• Get ready for a wonderful discovery!

Calm your breathing, relax your body and then take several slow, confident steps deep into your inner world.

Soon you will see a large box. It is magnificently wrapped, with a huge bow on top. Enjoy your feeling of anticipation.

Inside that box is an aspect of yourself that is laughing, spontaneous, playful; a part of yourself that is always willing to smile.

When you are ready, lift the lid of the box and allow your Laughing Self to emerge. Greet her or him with all the warmth you can. You have a friend for life. Ask for her name. Admire how she looks. Tell your Laughing Self you will call on her often and will cherish her. Listen to anything she has to say to you.

• Before your first meeting draws to a close, promise your Laughing Self how you will cherish her. Perhaps you will

—Smile often, enjoying the relaxation and openness that follows.

—Seek out situations where your capacity to be joyful can be nourished (clown workshops, shared 'foolish' activities, playing with children, singing, dancing to vibrant music).

—Prioritise time with people who are life-affirming.

—Put 'smiling reminders' around your house and at your place of work (these could include a drawing of your Laughing Self, or a message in her name).

—Ask a friend to do this meditation, then allow your two Laughing Selves to support each other as you review your progress regularly—with a smile!

Your Tree of Life

Drawing your Tree of Life can be illuminating at any time but especially when you feel churned up or out of contact with yourself. I sometimes combine this meditation with a request to my inner world to send me an image I can use in relation to the Tree. This is often a bird, sometimes a rainbow, once an umbrella neatly folded next to the Tree (my protection against storm?), and occasionally I have found myself drawing a figure I recognise as an aspect of myself which is 'apart' because I am neglecting it. The richness and variety of response provoked by this simple active meditation make it one of my favourites.

• Have a large sheet of paper ready and some crayons. Take time to move away from your daily concerns to focus on the idea that you are going to draw your Tree of Life.

• Draw quickly, spontaneously, without censorship or judgement. Draw for at least five minutes.

• If you do this active meditation with a friend, when you have finished drawing talk about what is on the page, speaking in the first person as though you are the Tree. 'I notice that my branches are bare . . . but my roots go far down into rich soil'; 'I am reaching up as high as I can yet there's still far to go before I reach the sky . . .'

If you do this active meditation alone, write your comments down in the first person, just as though you were speaking. Looking at yourself, symbolised in your drawing by the Tree, you might consider:

Am I a winter Tree; summery; with leaves or fruit; without?

Do I stand alone or are there other plants or trees nearby?

Where is my strength: branches, trunk, foliage?

Do my roots feel deep, well-nourished, fragile?

In what kind of soil do I stand?

Am I an old Tree or a new one?

Are there figures, birds or animals nearby?

Am I well cared for, or neglected; wild or tamed; native or imported?

What is the general feeling I convey?

Is there anything this Tree needs?

Drawing your Tree may take you on to think anew about an aspect of your life which is troubling you, yet you may not feel you have a particular insight right away. Don't worry. As with all your therapy drawing, remain open, curious. You can always return to it, continuing to write or speak in the first person. The key is to expect nothing, which is far more difficult than it sounds! However, expecting nothing, you avoid pushing for a preordained outcome which may be far from what you need or want to discover.

Franny said this after drawing her Tree.

'My left side has such droopy looking branches. Pathetic, they look somehow. Yet it is much heavier than my right . . . My left side is sore. Sore. Sad. I feel sad. I feel undernourished on that side of my body. Not since my Dad died has anyone given me a big hug that really touched and opened out my heart . . . I feel sad.'

Fully alive

- Calm your mind with slow, easy breaths. You are taking time away from your usual concerns, but will return to them refreshed.

When you are ready, close your eyes, slowly. Relax your shoulders, your arms, your hands, your face, your neck, your tongue.

- Feeling comfortable, and with your breathing continuing— easy, easy, in and out—take your mind back to a time when you felt fully alive. It could be a recent moment. Maybe it was years ago.

Recall that time with love and interest. Take pleasure in the aliveness you are recalling.

Stay with the scene for as long as you can, noticing what is happening outside yourself and inside also. Feel the atmosphere of that time: what was said, expressed; how people moved; how you responded or what you initiated.

When you feel the scene is leaving you, or you are leaving that scene, slowly come back to the present.

- Now write about that scene, recreating it on the page, noting your reactions and feelings. Write in the present tense: 'The sun is hot and I am full of excitement because today . . .'
- When you have finished writing, close your eyes and take

yourself back into the scene. This time, ask your inner world for an image that relates to the scene or encapsulates it for you. If a word arises, write that down. If it is a visual image, take time to draw it.

That word, or image, could be displayed in your room as a useful reminder to you how wonderful it feels to be fully alive, *and that you can feel that way*.

• With the scene still in your mind, explore these questions, jotting down your responses and allowing at least five minutes to muse and write on each one.

How could that intense feeling of aliveness be more generally available to you?

What stands between you and that fully alive experience of self?

Is there any small change that needs to take place *in you* before you can feel that aliveness as your usual state of being?

Exploring your myth of origin

Are you a black person living in a white-dominated country? Were you adopted by a family with a culture or religion different from your own? Maybe you had to flee your country of origin? Or have you always felt out of place with the family of your birth? This active meditation can help. Time, large sheets of paper, paint or brightly coloured crayons are needed. Play music you associate with peaceful, inward-turning thoughts.

• Using your paints or your crayons, begin slowly and curiously to unravel your personal myth of origin.

Look inwards for inspiration, hunches and feelings, rather than reaching outwards towards 'facts'. The style of drawing you choose is unimportant. The goal is not to come up with finished art for the framers but to allow feelings to emerge about where you have come from and where you belong or where you want to belong.

You might make a journey back through history, across continents, into the worlds of myth, of community; even to the beginning of time.

You might soak more deeply into a town or village or a specific community of like-minded people where you feel some sense of belonging.

You might move to an ideal land of your own creation.

• As your hand moves across the page, if a particular image arises, enjoy drawing it out—literally—on the page. If words arise, put them down!

Perhaps a single page is only a beginning. Tape a whole series of pages together as your myth emerges. Draw or paint until your feeling is one of satisfaction, or of being emptied out. Be playful, open, ready. Your mind is full of surprises.

You may want to find poems or quotes from writers that express your feelings about your origins. Add them to your drawing.

• Should you feel stuck, check out what is happening in the present.

Perhaps you feel silly. (Silly in whose eyes?)

Perhaps you can't draw. (Your myth can emerge anyway—or an image associated with the idea of a myth of origin.)

Perhaps you feel this active meditation won't get you anywhere. (Who says you shouldn't waste a little time?)

Perhaps you feel you belong nowhere, or have no sense of origin. Think about what you enjoy. Do you come from a long line of keen readers? Could you become part of the great family of builders, of cooks, of parents, of singers? Maybe you are a good talker, or listener. Could that lead you to a sense of community with others who have enjoyed those same pleasures?

Treasure your connections, *especially those which are self-created*.

False self

As an adult you can choose to express yourself as you want. Perhaps that option—and the sense of authenticity that accompanies it— was not available to you as a child or young person.

If you suspect you had to keep your thoughts and feelings to yourself, and present a rather different self to the outside world from the way you felt inside, it can help to write a letter to your parents or the people who were most powerful in your childhood. (As you will not send this letter, the exploration will be just as powerful if the people you are writing to are alive or dead.)

• Spend some time recalling the people you are writing to. Remember how they moved, spoke, smelt, felt; what made them laugh or cry; what caused them to get angry; what they valued.

• Now begin to write your letter.

Make it as detailed as possible. Use the letter—which you can write as many times as you want—to chart your transition from being the kind of person you were to the kind of person you are now.

Tell them what you believed you were not allowed to say, or think, or feel, or do that would have more genuinely or truthfully expressed who you are. Tell them how it felt to keep that inside.

There may have been some real satisfactions you got from keeping some things to yourself. You can share that now.

• Think about the person you were. Think about the person you are now.

Perhaps you are very different now from your child-self? Perhaps you have barely changed?

There is no judgement in either outcome, but use this time to discover what that particular journey has been like for you.

• When you have finished writing, take time to read what you have written.

Value the insights this letter-writing brings *but do not mail the letter!*

Only much later, when your emotions have settled and you have accepted responsibility for your life in the present, should you think of writing a quite different, less confronting letter. Or, better still, if they are alive, talk to your parents or those significant adults, *asking them how it was for them to be your parent*.

• If you find writing the letter difficult, or you feel uncomfortably stirred up, you may want to

—Light a bonfire of blaming (see p 115).

—Let your anger go (see p 195).

In his early forties, Martin lives in a household with several other adults and children. After several false starts, he wrote a long letter to his parents which expressed his deepest feelings. The letter was *never sent* but months after writing it he recognised he had let go much of his tension with his parents. Inevitably, they seemed more relaxed with him also.

Being yourself

Who are you living to please?

Who is directing your life?

Are you living a life that feels real?

Are you living a life of your own choosing?

Being true to yourself—being yourself—does not mean disregarding others. It does, however, demand awareness that you are the director of your own life. That can be hard to take on!

• Slow your breathing, relax your body. Check that you are comfortable. Take time to recall a situation when you were able to trust and be guided by your own inner sense of reality, and to act accordingly. It need not be a big event or a major situation; just one where you trusted your sense of what was right for you.

Write down any thoughts or feelings you have about that situation.

• Now recall a situation where you decided—for any reason—you had to follow maps and rules decided by other people.

What was that like? Recall and jot down the thoughts and feelings you had then. And now?

• Expand your awareness outwards from those two particular situations to discover whether you find it easier in some situations than others to be yourself, to know what you want, to act and behave truthfully. Take a recent week in your life as an example, re-running how you were in different situations: alone, with friends, at work, with authority figures, colleagues, with strangers.

Jot down your memories and impressions.

Are you able to 'borrow' a helpful insight from one area of your life and choose to apply it to another? ('With friends I'm less inclined to talk too much than with people I am trying to impress.' 'In carpentry class I can concentrate and lose myself in the work. That's what I want from my paid work also.')

If *being yourself* is a concept that is difficult or confusing, ask your Wise Being (see p 23) for a word or image to support you. Write that word down, or draw the image, and put it where you can see it often.

Take heart that all the active meditations in this book will increase your confidence about being yourself.

Living truthfully

'The Greek word for truth, alethea, means "not hidden".'
Catherine Kober, 'Shifting the pavement',
Free Associations, 10

'Living truthfully' does not mean telling everyone all that comes into your mind; nor that your life should be an open book. *Using your discretion about your confidences is absolutely valid.*

However, the suppression of an important truth about yourself in a relationship which matters creates tension and unease ('If she knew what I was really like, she couldn't love me.'). Also, 'living truthfully', it is possible to become surer of your motives. That means you enjoy a relatively clear sense of why you are acting as you are, and whether it is appropriate.

Here is a way to begin to explore what living truthfully might mean. Take it slowly if it stirs up painful memories. This exploration is intended to stretch over several self-therapy sessions.

• Make yourself comfortable. Should you feel restless, stand up and shake away your excess energy, then sit again.

• Spend at least fifteen minutes thinking about the way your family of origin functioned in relationship to truth. (This may be especially painful if someone in your family was an addict or an abuser and the rest of the family had to collude with their defences.)

Jot down thoughts and memories as they occur to you.

Write down the lies you believe were commonly told in your family. As you write them down, attend to your body, relaxing any uncomfortable tension, and checking that you are breathing deeply and slowly. *Take your time.*

• Recall if or when silence or even lies was preferred to the truth ('I would rather not know that you are angry, depressed, abused, gay, sick . . .'). This preference may have been expressed openly— or covertly through a family taboo. Do you have a sense of who was being protected, from what, and why? Jot down your memories, the feelings you recall and also the feelings you have now.

If you are distressed by your memories, stop here and take time to comfort the child you once were (see p 120).

• Perhaps in your family harsh truth-telling was used as a weapon ('I'm only telling you this for your own good . . .').

Such 'truth-telling' may have been a way to maintain power or distance. Could it also have been a consciously or unconsciously sadistic attempt to avoid pain by passing on pain?

Keep noting your memories, thoughts and feelings from the past and in the present. Draw any images that seem too strong or unwieldy to be put into words.

• Do you have any memories of an important truth being withheld from you? How did that feel then? How does it feel now? Would it help to talk about that either to the person involved or perhaps with someone who is willing to be an intimate listener (see p 196)?

• Are there situations now where it seems risky for you to tell the truth? Are there people you need to exaggerate to, or bluff? Are there things about yourself you fear showing, or speaking of?

Are you aware what you are saving yourself from?

Do your strategies work for you?

Would it be appropriate to act differently?

It may help to work with the fear exercises (see index), and then reconsider your feelings about truth-telling.

• When you feel you have understood old messages about truth-telling, make a decision about what kind of truth-teller you can afford to be now, and note that in your journal ('I'm ready to share with my lover why I am sometimes sexually withholding, but I do not want to discuss my lesbianism at work as it would cause me stress.').

Note too how much of the truth you can let others tell you—even when what they have to say may upset or hurt you.

• Remember, you can practise speaking the truth, and hearing the truth spoken, in a safe environment: with yourself in the experience of Free Writing and Free Drawing; through Intimate listening (see p 196), or by writing a letter *which you do not post* (see p 113).

Don't hesitate to ask your Wise Being (see p 23) for a word or an image to help if you feel stuck, overwhelmed or depressed.

Your sense of self under attack

For most people, a personal attack hurts. It hurts when it comes at you directly: 'You have to be one of the most contemptible people I have ever met'; 'I find your body disgusting'. It hurts when it is sly and covert: 'My children never tried that with me'; 'Your voice certainly does rise above the crowd'; 'I'm sure you were doing your best, but . . .'.

The sad thing is how we brood upon critical attacks, while approving remarks can so easily be shrugged aside. The explanation lies with our capacity to do ourselves down. This in turn comes from too little self-love and self-acceptance, itself a result of attacks on our being, usually when we are most vulnerable—in childhood.

Here is a way to learn to see personal attacks for what they are, and to be rather less vulnerable to them.

• Recall a recent or important time when you felt attacked or criticised. Run that scene though your mind: what happened; how it felt.

Now re-run it much more slowly, this time holding in your conscious awareness the knowledge that a passionate or viperish attack describes not you but *the attacker's state of mind*.

How does that knowledge shift your perception of the event? Jot down any thoughts or feelings you may have.

• Recall what your strategy was when under attack (defence, tears, anger, depression?). Now run the scene through in your mind yet again, this time noting that the attack reflects the attacker, and not the truth of who you are.

Engaging with an attacker is rarely helpful. You will find yourself defending your integrity in a way that should not be necessary.

Re-run the scene a last time and rehearse your relative passivity in the face of such an attack (a hearty shrug can help!).

• Resolve to increase your self-protection in one of the following ways.

1 Deflecting insults (see p 81).
2 Reviewing what you know and trust about yourself (see p 223).
3 Moving from fear to love (see p 221).

Your strategy may not positively affect the attacker, but it will allow you to feel more flexible and compassionate, and to retain your sense of integrity.

Resisting attacking others

This active meditation should not be done without first exploring Your sense of self under attack (see above).

• Settle yourself comfortably. Ask yourself if you are ready to look at a few emotional home truths without wallowing in self-blame.

• Think over your conduct with others during the last week or month. Take time to become aware of when and why *you attack others*.

It will help to re-run an actual situation in your mind. Jot down your memories, thoughts and feelings. Write down your excuses also. ('As rude as that woman was, anyone would have done what I did. And more. She got off lightly.')

Try to get some sense as to whether you make your attacks directly or covertly. (Some people attack while smiling. Are you one of them?)

• Thinking back over those events, explore what response you were after. Did you get the response you wanted? If it was attention, or revenge, or a release of tension or something else you have identified, is there some other way you could get that same satisfaction?

Take time to consider your desired response. It is confronting, and you may find it difficult at first.

• Now explore carefully what emotions *preceded* your attack; what emotional buttons had been pushed; what your state of mind was.

Don't look for fresh excuses here, but it is helpful to know if there are triggers you can learn to recognise. You can then choose to react or act differently. Jot down your thoughts and feelings.

• Now run the scene through again in your mind. Visualise yourself getting ready to attack, *but instead, using your self-awareness to find out what is behind your wish to hurt someone else.* (It could be hurt feelings, pain, fear, contempt, envy, intolerance, etc.)

Rehearse

—Turning away from the person and the potential conflict.

—Watching your thoughts (see pp 41, 81).

—Using aware breathing as respite ('Breathing in I calm my body. Breathing out, I smile'.).

Later, and it may be only moments later, you can speak to the person about what is actually troubling you, rather than impulsively trying to do them down.

• Next time you are hot to attack, or have attacked, review that process: how it worked for you; whether you need to give more time to this issue; what your ideal outcome would be; what lies between you and that ideal outcome.

Not playing persecutor

Has it ever happened that someone is telling you a story that carries some emotional weight and you hear yourself commenting or cutting them off in a way that denies the emotional content of what you have just been told?

If you do not feel good about yourself, it is only too easy to take advantage of someone else's vulnerability to release feelings of hostility or even sadism. Women as well as men do this, but men may more often deny their hostility under the poisonous guise of 'rational thinking and responding'.

• Recall a recent situation when you were unable to listen empathically, or when someone else's pain stimulated you to attack, deny or express contempt.

What was going on *for you* at that time? Recall both outer events and inner feelings.

Was your response dominated by your personal memories of previous painful encounters with that same person, or with a different person in a similar situation? Could you now acknowledge a lack of freshness in your response?

What did you hope to gain from the response you gave? Did that work for you? For the other person?

• With a clearer sense of what *you were expressing about yourself* in that encounter, formulate a different strategy for a similar encounter in the future.

Acknowledge what form your hostility is likely to take: you will feel tempted to set the other person straight; you will want to inform them their problems are exaggerated, unreal, unimportant; you will want to talk about yourself; you will want to tell them they are crazy.

Now promise yourself *that you will keep your thoughts to yourself.*

Silence is preferable to a hurtful comment. Or select and practise an innocuous remark ('You poor old thing', 'It sounds terrible').

Only when emotions have settled is it appropriate to suggest a 'rational' review of the situation. But ask yourself: are you doing it for the other person's sake, or to affirm your superiority?

• Having reviewed your possibilities and formulated a brief strategy, rehearse it in your mind. How does it feel for you? How will it leave the other person feeling? Do you have a sense of ease rather than conflict?

• Once you are happy with what you have decided, anchor this new strategy by formulating it into a brief practical sentence or two and writing it in your journal. Promise yourself, too, that when a desire to attack others arises in your mind, you will take time to ask: What is happening in me, right now? What am I needing, right now?

Formulate that promise into a sentence also, and write it— conspicuously—in your journal.

Feeling guilty

Many people have a vague feeling of guilt which hovers much of the time, occasionally finding something specific to attach to, at other times seeming unfathomable but no less real.

It is possible to explore what is lying behind the guilt.

Perhaps you feel confused about self-responsibility, or responsibility for others.

Perhaps it is hard to trust that others can take care of themselves.

Perhaps guilt is protecting you from the need to act and finding the courage to act.

Perhaps what you call guilt is actually self-pity which is, in turn, shielding and shadowing an urge to get attention in a more positive way.

• Use Free Writing (see p 32) to understand those feelings of guilt and the deeper issues which may lie behind them.

Take as your guiding sentence: 'I feel guilty about . . .'; 'I feel guilty because . . .'; 'I feel guilty when . . .'.

Gradually you will recognise a pattern to your guilt feelings.

Then you can begin to use your self-knowledge and awareness to discriminate where
—Guilt is a shield for a need or emotion that is even less acceptable to your conscious mind (hatred, contempt, fear, pity, sadness), or where
—Guilt is the product of generalised anxiety, or of habitual over or under-involvement in other people's lives.
• When you are ready, take your time to decide on a shift in behaviour or response that will allow fresh, more appropriate responses to replace the guilt-laden responses from the past. Perhaps an emotion can now emerge that will serve you better than guilt?

Remind yourself that following a shift in awareness, and in your thinking, *will also come a change in feelings*.
• Formulate a simple strategy and note it in your journal. Then you can give yourself more support as that is needed. You may find it useful to turn to
—Women should/Men should (see p 96).
—Loosening up on resentment (see p 101).
—Not getting what you want (see p 232).

Taking criticism

The following meditation addresses an issue which is touchy or painful in many lives.

Being able to 'take criticism' is generally regarded as some kind of virtue. Certainly it is an asset to be able to assess what criticism is useful and what is not, and to know that it is your behaviour, feelings or what you are doing that is being criticised and not your deepest self. But your response to criticism is not always entirely within your immediate, conscious control.

Where there has been lots of unconditional love, it is easier to grow up able to take criticism. When most of what you did was admired by other people, it becomes easier to take criticism. When you have felt confident about how you appeared in other people's eyes, it is easier to shrug off criticism.

However, if you grew up in a family—as many people did and do—where adult criticism of children was constant, where praise was in short supply, where teachers scolded more than encouraged, where it seemed that everything you did offended someone, then you might feel you have used up a lifetime's capacity to take criticism and not be crushed by it. Let this meditation help you.

• Settle into a mood of quiet anticipation. Steady your breathing. Check that your body is comfortable.

• Recall a recent or especially hurtful time when you were criticised (fairly or unfairly—it doesn't matter). Recall your feelings, how you defended yourself, how you felt later. Write down those memories and what your feelings are now.

• Cast your mind back to your childhood, perhaps to the year you turned twelve. Recall the atmosphere of your home, and of school. Jot down anything you can remember about patterns of affirmation and/or criticism in your family of origin, at school, at your church or at any clubs or organisations you belonged to. What were your strategies as a child to defend yourself from criticism?

It can help to recall particular events and see yourself reacting.

• Now use Free Writing (see p 32) to explore the issue even more deeply. Your guiding sentence could be: 'I resent criticism because . . .' or 'When I am criticised I feel . . .'.

• Once you have a clearer picture of how your history affects your responses in the present, you can begin to shift those attitudes so you are less vulnerable. You can begin by learning to discriminate between criticism that feels helpful and criticism that feels crushing.

• Recall two specific incidents that reflect those different styles of criticism. (Usually people can take criticism more easily from someone who has their interests at heart, or where there are clear common interests to be addressed—in the workplace, for example.)

• Now visualise yourself being criticised fairly, or constructively. Rehearse your awareness that this is not an attack on yourself.

Note what you feel.

• Finally, visualise yourself being criticised unfairly. Rehearse some strategies that will help you. These may include

—Deflecting insults (see p 81).

—Asserting your self (see p 85).

—Refusing negative projections (see p 206).

If your strategy fails the first few times, or the first few hundred times, take it as an opportunity to go on revising what you know and trust about yourself, and moving on.

Criticising others

In the way you criticise others, you express much about the way you feel about yourself. When you have fully explored Taking criticism (see above), it is worth doing more truth-probing to explore whether you use criticism as an expression of power, envy, or as self-protection.

• Recall a recent situation in which you criticised someone else. Remember what your body conveyed, what tone of voice and words you used, what message lay behind your words.

Jot down your thoughts and feelings. Maybe there is an image of your criticising self you could draw and then dialogue with (see p 31).

• Return to your memories of the encounter and try to recall what you wanted to achieve through your criticism? Did you get what you wanted?

Go deeper than your first reactions. Take time to write and withdraw, write and withdraw.

• Recalling that encounter again, as though in the present, are there ways you could tone down your criticisms, or make them more constructive?

Perhaps you feel stuck, wondering how to do that?

Ask your inner world for an image or a word to help you. It may be a ticking clock, reminding you to give yourself time before reacting so your approach can soften and be more constructive.

Consciously acknowledge that *criticism should be of actions or behaviour only; never of the person's being, beliefs, appearance or body.* This is true of criticism in the home (to partners and children) as well as in more public, neutral encounters. Jot down your thoughts about that, and especially how this insight might affect any future encounters.

Rehearse how you can make a statement *in the first person* and *about your own reaction.*

Rather than 'You're always so depressed these days,' you might say, 'I notice that you are depressed and I don't know what to do.'

Instead of 'You drive me crazy with your whining,' you might say, 'When I hear a whine in your voice I feel angry instead of open with you.'

• You may need to consider how much you expect of another person. Are your demands unreal or inappropriate? If you don't know, take the time to check with the person involved. You may then need to find ways to compromise or back off.

• Rehearse making appropriate interventions in your self-therapy sessions. Remember you can help yourself by Asking for what you want (see p 231) and Borrowing the behaviour you need (see p 62).

Perhaps your problem is not criticising, but feeling that you can never criticise or speak out, *even when that is appropriate.*

Assertiveness training can help; so can conflict resolution. Both teach skills to help the person who under-reacts as much as the person who over-reacts (see p 85).

Deflecting insults

Someone insults you, derides or belittles you. Someone deflates your triumph. Someone smiles as they tell you something unpleasant about a person you love, or as they denigrate a project you care about.

• Watch their words. Watch them glide by as you have learned to watch your own thoughts go by (see p 41).

Watch how those words sag when you don't give them energy to land or even hover.
• Remind yourself who is watching those words without agitation or defensiveness.
It is your self.

Let's suppose you rehearse this active meditation in a self-therapy session and like it. However, next time someone insults you, you spring to your own defence, following a long-established habit, or you cry, or feel depressed. Take that experience as an opportunity to return to this meditation. You may need to use visualisation many times before your old habits weaken and lie down. But they will! And you will benefit greatly.
• Visualise again letting the hurtful insult pass by. See it moving past you, rather than invading you. Notice as you do so how your body feels and what your feelings are. Take pleasure in the energy you are saving for worthier causes.
• Now remind yourself what you know, like or trust about yourself. Even a modest claim to self-love will do. Add to it every day (see p 223).

Decision-making

Do you know what weight you are giving to decision-making in serious and relatively petty areas of your life?

Take a slow-moving self-therapy session to reflect on the way you make decisions. At the end of the session you may want to make a new decision about how to make decisions! Or you may want to read Just standing (see p 143). Either way, you will have more insight.
• Review the following questions, taking at least ten minutes for each as you write; withdraw to think more deeply; write again, then withdraw.

Are you able to make decisions? Are there some areas in your life where decision-making is impossible? Do you want to change that?

Are you inclined to make decisions for people other than yourself?

Do you worry as much about small decisions (beans or broccoli for dinner) as over bigger ones (a new language, or computer skills) or major ones (shall I leave my partner whom I no longer love)?

Do you make decisions actively or passively?

A few years ago a friend came to Sydney. She was here for only a couple of days from the small town where she lives. How did she choose to spend her time? Looking for oriental carpets. Such carpets are cheaper and more varied here. She has a large, graceful house and takes pride in its beauty. But it is possible to wonder if she had decided, actively, to spend her time rolling and unrolling carpets, and discussing prices, or if she found herself doing so, and only later thought—or maybe not—about all that lay outside the carpet warehouses.

• Notice when you are driven (by what, by whom?) to certain decisions.

If you are making decisions you despise, has the time come to change that process? Listening. Just listening (see p 257) could help.

Sleep on it (see below) also allows you to deepen your understanding of how and when you take conscious responsibility.

• When change is needed, formulate your resolve into a brief, practical sentence. Write that in your journal and *make a decision* to follow it up.

Sleep on it

My children go to a Rudolf Steiner school where the children are taught the day's key learning during what is called the Main Lesson. I was interested to discover that the children do not write in response to what they hear and learn on the same day, but that instead *they sleep on it*, then return to the previous day's lesson the next day, to remember, talk, write and draw about it—before moving on to the next stage of the Main Lesson, *and the next round of sleeping on it*.

Many adults feel under extreme pressure to respond immediately to whatever situation they are in. Perhaps they feel unable to tolerate uncertainty. Perhaps they feel a fast response accords with these hectic times. Yet *sleeping on it* can add depth and clarity to decision-making. Jung recognised this when he said that with some problems it was 'better to let them develop their own inner resolution'.

Could offering yourself the chance 'to sleep on it' shift the pace and style of your thinking and decision-making?

• Recall three decisions you have made during the last year.

Write down what the choices were—and also what you decided.

Jot down what you now think about the outcome in each case, with the benefit of hindsight.

• Did you make those decisions to please yourself, to please others, or in a way acceptable to yourself *and* anyone else involved?

What resources did you feel able to call on (experience, advice, a sense of appropriate timing)?

Do you have more resources now (meditating, Wise Being, stronger sense of self)?

• Recall the time frame of those decisions. Did it suit you? Were you affected by an imposed time frame?

What would an ideal time frame be for you?

• Visualise yourself making similar decisions in the future. Consider if you could be helped by

—Taking the decision-making process more slowly.

—Talking with your Wise Being.

—Asking your inner world for a dream to guide you.

• Note any simple, practical resolution you want to make.

Sleep well!

Asserting your self

'Broadly speaking, self-assertion takes two forms: the conscious reaching out for what one wants and the conscious rejection of what one doesn't want.'

Alexander Lowen, *The Betrayal of the Body*

This active meditation may be especially useful to women who are highly tuned to meeting the needs of other people and who may sometimes have more difficulty feeling clear about what they themselves want—or are entitled to.

The following are all vital expressions of a steady sense of self.

—Learning to identify what you want.

—Distinguishing between what is important (life-enhancing) to have, and what is not.

—Feeling able to tolerate frustration.

—Feeling entitled to take in and 'have' what is available to you.

—Knowing that it is possible to act with consideration for others, without acting *only to please others*.

—Feeling that it is 'safe' to say no when to say yes would be untrue to your sense of self.

• Spend several minutes thinking about each of these points and evaluating them in relation to what you know about your own reactions, hesitations and behaviour.

It will help to remember specific situations or encounters. As you do so, avoid making harsh judgements. What you are looking for are areas of your life which need your attention and creativity.

Jot down your thoughts and feelings. Take at least fifteen minutes to write, withdraw to think; write, withdraw.

• Over a month or so, use your journal to explore your feelings that day about *reaching out for what you want* and *consciously rejecting what you do not want*.

Where one or other aspect feels weak or underdeveloped—or dangerous—continue working on this issue in your self-therapy sessions. Here's how you could do this.

Picture yourself in a real-life situation that has been difficult or disappointing, but now in your fantasy you are acting in a way that seems true to your sense of self and to what you want. How does that feel? Is there any hurdle or hesitation that still needs attention?

Remind yourself that respecting other people includes respecting their capacity to take care of themselves, and to tolerate frustration. (Your saying no may inconvenience someone, perhaps even hurt them momentarily, but it is unlikely to do them lasting damage.) Does that seem like an insight that's difficult to put into action? Decide what might help. *Rehearse your strategy in the safety of your self-therapy session.*

• Ask your Wise Being (see p 23) for help with saying no, or yes, or both. You can also ask your Wise Being or your inner world for a visual image to strengthen you. This could be a Cloak of Courage, or a talisman of some other kind. You will receive the image you need. Use it often.

If saying no, or yes, continues to be a problem for you, consider assertiveness training. This can clarify strategies for you. It can teach you to say no without undue anxiety, and to be clear when it is appropriate to say yes. Assertiveness training is available in most major cities and usually involves working in a group, with an assertiveness training leader, over a series of four to six meetings.

Dissolving the barriers

The more secure you are as a self, the less you will need to promote and guard your ego, and the more the barriers between your self and others can dissolve into meaninglessness. This does not mean there are no distinctions between you and other people, and other forms of life. There are. What it means is that these distinctions come to matter less, then finally not at all.

When you feel confident that you are on 'safe ground inside yourself' and that you are ready to do so, try the following meditation. Take it slowly. It should not be rushed into (or out of), but it can help you build a sense of connectedness, renew your sense of compassion, and strengthen your resolve to act in the face of injustice.

You may want to pre-record the instructions on a tape.

• Take time to settle yourself. Close your eyes. Slow your breathing. You are going to take a safe and rewarding journey, surrounded always with the protection of a golden, healing light.

• In your mind's eye, appreciate your body as it exists. Pat your outer edge, allowing yourself to be conscious that you are in your own body.

• Now, gradually allow your sense of your body's edge to feel less distinct than usual. As you imagine your body's edge becoming fuzzy or less distinct, continue to see yourself surrounded by the golden light which can extend as far as it is needed.

• Slowly feel yourself expanding beyond the edges of your body, still within the protection of the golden light. Your breathing is easy. You feel calm and happy, knowing that at any moment you can return to the safety and comfort of your normal boundaries.

• If you wish to do so, allow the expansion outside your usual experience of self gently to continue, always keeping yourself surrounded by golden, healing light.

You can expand your awareness to encompass the room in which you sit.

It is part of your consciousness.

You can expand your awareness to take in the building where you live, those you live with or near, your neighbourhood, and all who live there.

They are part of your consciousness.

You can expand your awareness to take in your town or city and all who live there.

They are part of your consciousness.

You can expand your awareness to take in your entire country with its rich and poor, its loved and unloved.

They are part of your consciousness.

You can expand your awareness to take in your planet—north, south, east, west—with its old and young, its loved and unloved.

They are part of your consciousness.

You can expand your awareness to experience how all of life is interconnected.

You are life. Life is in you. That is part of your consciousness.

Now you can experience that connection in your deepest being. Stay in that place, gently, calmly, within the infinite golden, healing light.

• When you are ready to do so, and from wherever you have allowed your awareness to travel, slowly bring your awareness back, remembering all the stages through which you have passed: life, planet, country, town, neighbourhood, those you live with or near, home, room, surrounded always, as you return to yourself, with protective golden light.

• Finally, again remind yourself:

I am here, in my town.

I am here, in my room.

I am here, in my body.

• With your awareness fully back in your body, again pat your body around the edges, appreciating it, loving it.

Breathe in. Breathe out.

• Then, slowly, open your eyes, look around you, stretch, shake out your limbs and resume your day.

Later, draw or write about your experience and any insights you had from this experience of connection.

PART TWO

Women and Men

'Whatever or whoever your self is, it is mediated
through a body which signals female or male and,
for most of your life, through characteristics of
behaviour, emotional response and attitude largely
associated with that body. Gender is difficult,
perhaps impossible, to escape; nowhere is this more
true than in our closest and most self-revealing
relationships.'

Intimacy and Solitude

Introduction

Moving through this section of the *Self-Therapy Book* you can increase your awareness about how you experience your gender, and how that supports or diminishes the way you want to be and feel when you are alone as well as when you are with other people. With that increased awareness will come an enlivened sense of new possibilities. You will be able to

—Separate out the 'shoulds' of the past from your desires in the present.

—Be true to who you are and relatively free from gender or sexual injunctions about how you should be—as a woman or man.

—'Borrow' freely and creatively from the gender which is not your own.

Taking responsibility for yourself and the environment you create around you; freeing yourself from the temptation to blame the past, your gender or the opposite sex for the ways in which your life is less than ideal; exploring ways of allowing other people—including partners and children—to express themselves more freely: those key therapeutic issues are also addressed and explored in the active meditations and exercises which follow.

You will make some serious discoveries, or maybe discoveries you can take seriously, but you will benefit by sometimes approaching these self-therapy sessions in a mood near to playfulness. Gender is, after all, something that few of us fully understand. It is also an area of life which is arguably more plastic than any other, at least in later life, and it is an area of life where fantasy and lived experience are in constant flux and flow.

Being a girl/a boy was like this . . .

Having some sense of how the atmosphere of your childhood shaped your experience of gender builds a bridge of understanding between the child-you and adult-you. It also clarifies why or how you may be reinforcing gender stereotypes in others—especially your own children.

An eminent psychologist who works with adolescents recently told me how he heard himself say to his twelve-year-old son who had fallen, 'Get up and stop crying. You're being a sissy.' He was obviously mortified by having done so. Even in the retelling there was a lot of passion in his words, but the words had leapt to his lips faster than his thoughts could censor them.

• In a page, or less, write—fast and without censorship—how it was for you being a male child or a female child. All the nonsense, the absurdity, the privileges, the frustrations—or as many of them as you can squeeze into a page! Use as your guiding sentence 'As a boy . . .' or 'As a girl . . .'.

• Move to a fresh page and recall as many of the commands, instructions and warnings you received as a child which particularly related to your 'correct' expression of gender. Write those down too, as many of them as you can: from home, school, parents, relatives, sports coaches, teachers.

It may help to see yourself as a child, perhaps dressed in school uniform or wearing child's clothes. Now listen for the voices that came down to your ears!

• Perhaps it was important to your parents that you were a particular kind of girl or boy. Recall what was especially emphasised in your family (modesty, conformity, acquiescence, helpfulness, success, competitiveness, silence).

Later you may want to circle words or phrases which strike you as key.

inside
freedom
imagination
dirty
nice girls
Mum's tired
girls' schools
If Dad said so
money

Those words or injunctions may continue to ring in your life today, perhaps in more muted or complex forms. Be clear what they are, and *how you now want to hear them.*

• You can explore any individual word or injunction at greater depth, using Free Writing (see p 32) or Free Drawing (see p 30). Use as your guiding sentence, 'Writing the word _____, I feel . . .' or, 'Writing the word _____, I remember . . .'.

Draw any associations you have to a particular word or phrase (detention, nice girls) or an image that arises when you remember your child-self.

• Note in your journal if there are any resolutions you want to make to free you from the shadow of the child other people needed you to be.

Breaking rules

Was there something special that as a child you were not allowed to do because you were the 'wrong' sex for the particular experience? Now is your chance!

• Settle comfortably. Close your eyes. Roll your eyes backwards, and then relax them down, breathing out as you do so. Relax your face, your tongue. Breathe easily.

• Recall a time when you were angry or upset because you wanted to do something and you couldn't do it because only girls did that, or only boys.

You were furious, and also powerless.

Now you are not powerless.

Now you can return to that time and have the outcome you wanted.

There will be no ill-effects as you break the rules. No one will punish you or mock you or laugh at you.

Perhaps you were a girl who always wanted to wear trousers to school so you could climb to the top of the climbing frame and hang upside down for longer than anyone else. Now you can.

Perhaps you wanted to help Dad take the car to pieces. In your imagination, your hands are already covered with grease. The pieces of the engine are spread on a dirty blanket and you can see exactly which bits to hand Dad when he mutters his instructions.

Perhaps you were a boy who always wanted to play with Barbies. In this fantasy, all boys love playing with Barbies. They play with them for hours, changing their clothes, giving them a bath, brushing their hair and chatting about them with their friends. Or perhaps you wanted to learn to sew and knit. In your mind's eye, see the garments you are making. Enjoy them, admire them. Show them to the other boys who are enjoying sewing with you.

• Only when you have had more than enough pleasure, open your eyes, breathe easily, and come back to the present.

• Choose to acknowledge that as an adult *you have choices that you didn't have as a child*. Can some of those childhood longings be transformed into adult pleasures?

• Use your journal to note your reactions to this active meditation, and to make any small resolutions that inspire you, or will increase your sense of gender freedom in the present.

The kind of woman/man I am . . .

Continue to uncover any limitations on the way you experience gender. It is possible to learn from this exercise, and it is easy to have fun with it, because you are thinking here about yourself at one remove, as a type, as a 'kind of . . .' rather than as the specific individual you are.

• Settle comfortably into a mood of open-minded discovery.

You are going to think about what kind of woman you are, or what kind of man you are, knowing that affects the way you think about your own self, and also affects the way that other people experience you.

• Use Free Writing (see p 32) to go beyond your normal assumptions, repeating, when your imagination falters, your guiding sentence: 'The kind of woman I am . . .' or 'The kind of man I am . . .'

Here is an example from Victor who found his discoveries rather galling as they did not quite fit his everyday view of himself, nor the view he wanted his lover to have of him. But that truthfulness of discovery is the point here.

'The kind of man I am never makes a mistake. Is always fit. Likes to have money in the bank. Is faithful but thinks about other women sexually. The kind of man I am is often randy. Wants to be seen as a hero. Will always stop when a motorist has broken down. Has mixed feelings about women's rights. Finds it hard to trust other men but prefers their company. Loves the pub. Hates housework. Plans continuous golf-playing in retirement.'

• Observe what you have written with curiosity and interest but with minimal judgement. There is still time to become the woman or man you want to be.

The kind of woman/man I admire is . . .

Take several moments to remind yourself you are leaving your daily concerns behind to explore a gentle fantasy. Ensure you are comfortable. Take a few slow, relaxing breaths.

• Think about the kind of woman you admire, or the kind of man. (Choose your own gender first. You can swap at a later session.) There may be a particular individual who comes into your mind. This could be a real person, an idealised person, a mythological being or someone from a book, play or film.

Look hard at the person. See her or him in various situations. Identify as precisely as you can just what it is you admire.

Write down your thoughts and observations, then withdraw to consider more deeply; write and withdraw; write and withdraw.

• When you have nothing left to add, look over what you have written.

Circle the qualities you think are important.

Are those qualities generally admired in our society *or genuinely admired by you*? Either way is fine, but it's useful to be clear.

Could the kind of woman or man you admire possibly exist, with all the conflicts and disappointments and contradictions that are part of human life?

• Without self-blame or judgement, reflect on where there are gaps between the kind of woman or man you presently are, and the kind of woman or man you admire. Write down whatever your feelings are about that gap. Decide if there is anything you can do to bring yourself closer to being the kind of woman or man you admire. You would be supported by Meditating on the qualities you most desire (see pp 145–6) and Borrowing the behaviour you need (see p 62).

Women should/men should

Free Writing (see p 32) can help you explore the gender imperatives, finding out how deeply these are rooted in your sense of self.

No one will observe what you write, and the exercise will help you as long as you don't censor to please an imagined observer. It will be illuminating to discover that in the back of your up-to-the-minute mind a voice may be saying *a husband should earn more money than his wife*, or maybe *women should keep talk of menstruation to themselves*, *women should wait to be approached sexually* or *men ought to be able to act fearlessly*.

• Take a few minutes to settle in to a mood of relaxed discovery, open-minded and curious. Resolve to write for at least fifteen minutes, withdrawing to think; writing; withdrawing; writing. Take as your guiding phrases 'Women should . . .' and 'Women ought . . .' (later you can substitute 'men' for 'women' or vice versa to explore the other gender). Follow the guiding phrases closely, as they will keep your mind focused.

• When you have finished writing, read through your 'shoulds' and take at least the same time to listen for the voices which accompany them. Some you will readily track back to your parents' injunctions, or to prevailing social ideas from the time you were growing up. Others may be more recent.

• Now compare those 'shoulds' to your current *conscious* attitudes. Where there are differences, decide whether the imperatives have served their purpose. Are you ready to let them go?

If you are ready to let them go, write a sentence or two that expresses that, and then read it aloud ('It's a drag Damien won't climb on the roof but I'm afraid of heights myself. I am willing to accept neither of us is especially brave.').

With the imperatives you feel uneasy about but are not ready to give up, acknowledge them for what they are: *part* of your thinking, *part* of your feelings, *part* of your beliefs. They are not *who you are*.

• Where those imperatives directly affect another person ('I still blame Maeve for being an angry mother.'), choose to spend your next self-therapy sessions exploring two meditations which will help you to see yourself and the other person a little differently: Unconditional love (see p 165) and Not getting what you want (see p 232). A trade-off may also be possible, if both people are willing. This is explained on p 179.

Women can: I can/men can: I can

Here is another exercise to have fun with! It is also one you can share with a partner or friends.

• Take a few moments to move your awareness away from your daily life. Visualise a light turned on in your head that will allow you to see things in a fresh and creative way.

• Spend at least fifteen minutes exploring to find out if there is anything you want to do—or feel—which until now you believed could *only* be done or felt by the opposite sex. Visualise the opposite sex socially, within the family, in the workplace; at recreational pursuits; as a parent or as an adult child. Take your time. Those are varied areas of life to consider. As any ideas occur to you about what you have been missing out on, jot them down.

• Now ask yourself who or what has kept you from acting or feeling across the whole range of gender activity? Jot down whatever comes to your mind.

Does anything stop you now? Note what it is—if anything— then resolve momentarily to set any obstacle to one side.

• Decide if you are willing to try something new—first in fantasy only, then, when it feels safe and appropriate, in real life.

Choose from one of those behaviours or activities you believed was available only to the opposite sex but which you would like for yourself.

Envisage yourself behaving, feeling or acting in this new way.

Savour the experience for as long as possible, then describe in writing how it was for you. You might also want to notice your resistances. Are those resistances a challenge to you?

• Make a note in your journal to remind yourself to return to this fantasy until you feel ready to try out something new in your everyday life, and so extend your choice of behaviours.

• When you have made that decision, frame it as a resolve that you can write down in your journal and feel strengthened by ('I now feel ready to take time away from the family without compensating for my absence in advance.'). Make time to review your progress from fantasy to 'real life'. Be sensitive to where you must continue to give yourself support.

Heterosexuals can/Lesbians or gay men can . . .

This active meditation follows the same steps as those outlined in the previous meditation, Women can: I can. This time you switch your awareness to those whose sexual choice is different from your own. Like that meditation, it can be fun to do—and strengthening. You may well discover that in thinking afresh about others' sexual choice, you are pushed to think anew about your own.

A word of caution is needed. In moving from fantasy to trying out new behaviours, be careful to negotiate with your loved one before any dramatic change takes place. (Your male partner may not cope at once with the idea of being 'dominated' when he has always 'led' sexually. Your female partner may be disturbed if you want to borrow and wear her clothes or make-up without discussion of what this means to you. Your lesbian lover may not want to 'role-play' just because it is an arousing fantasy for you.) This does not mean that change is not possible—on the contrary. But it does mean that out of respect for the other person, and their individuality, any change should be presented thoughtfully and with a real interest in what the other person also wants. Intimate listening can help (see p 196).

Resenting women/resenting men

A particular incident or person may justify our resentment, but carrying resentment about half the human race can be a costly burden. You can vary this active meditation, depending on the issues in your life. Perhaps it's the opposite sex you have least time and patience for? Perhaps it is your own?

• Choose whether you are focusing on women or men. (You can switch later.) Bring to mind a recent or lingering situation where actual women or men left you feeling resentful. Write down a brief description of that event.

• Now consider how your resentment in that particular situation was fuelled (or not) by the more general feelings of resentment you may have about women (or men). Write down all your resentments: behaviours, feelings, body language, attitudes, assumptions. None of it needs to be fair. Take at least thirty minutes, remembering and writing; writing and remembering.

• When you have nothing left to add, re-read what you have written and note what feelings emerged as you were remembering and writing (anger, sadness, despair, hilarity?).

Perhaps there is an image for those feelings that you want to draw. Or an image for the resentment itself. Take as much time as you need to draw your image and then to talk to it, asking it how you could resent a little less and feel somewhat more flexible some of the time.

• You may feel stuck with the resentment. If so, ask yourself, or your image, if you have one, *what small change needs to take place within you* to shift that resentment a little to let more complex feelings emerge. Remember, you cannot change other people—only your own attitude towards them.

Feel free to take this resentment to your Wise Being (see p 23) for help in understanding *what change is needed in you* to ease your burden of resentment.

Zahra said, 'My father and brothers are selfish pigs. Then I found myself married to another and working for yet one more! After I did the resentment meditation—when I drew an image of a big pig and tucked them all inside—I resolved to stick up for myself at home a little better and also to go back to a job (nursing) where I can work with more women than men. As it happens, some of the male nurses I work with are not pigs, and that's helped to defuse my all-men-are-pigs attitudes.'

Harriet said, 'I don't like women's company, but when I began to write down what I resent about women the list didn't add up to much and I could see it's more of an attitude than a reality.'

Loosening up on resentment

Resentment can block the feeling and expression of more positive emotions. You may well be absolutely entitled to your resentment, even while knowing it's doing you little good. The complex feelings lying behind resentment are often best uncovered using your body and breath as your allies.

Try this exploring exercise when you are in the house alone. You may want to make a lot of noise. Before you begin, read through the instructions. They are very simple and you don't want to be stopping to check out what to do next. If you find yourself doing this active meditation in some other way—your own way—that will be just fine.

• Make a big pile of cushions, or crouch on a bed.

Think of the person or an occasion that triggers your resentment. Don't force the memories. You might simply want to use a sentence which describes your attitude.

'I can't stand the way you make me your dumping ground.'

'I despise your drugs and your lies.'

'I am sick of being tolerant.'

• As you speak—and what you say may quickly change—hit the bed or the pile of cushions.

As you hit, *stretch out your arms and allow your chest to open*.

Continue hitting and speaking loudly—even shouting. If you feel silly, remind yourself no one is there to see you. Shout. Hit. Shout. Hit. 'It's not fair, Mum.' 'I hate my boss who got me sacked.'

Exhale your breath in big puffs.

• Keep your arms stretched out *as though hitting away from your body*.

• Continue hitting and shouting for as long as you can, or until you feel the release of emotions. You may find yourself crying, or feeling lost and empty. Don't rush to push those feelings away. Stay with them until they subside.

• Only after your feelings have settled, write whatever you need to in your journal. Don't analyse the experience. Simply note how you felt during the exploration, and now.

Sometimes you will release other feelings: shame, grief, loss, pity. Or you may re-experience old resentment from the past which you were unable to express appropriately at the time.

• If you want to continue to hit, try shouting as you do so, 'I'm letting it go. I'm letting it go.'

• Take time to calm your mind and feelings before returning to your occupations for the day.

Perhaps no emotions are released and you feel the exercise is entirely mechanical for you. Be patient with that, while knowing that holding onto resentment—or letting it swamp you and other people—is never helpful. You can return to the exercise whenever you choose.

Appreciating women/appreciating men

It's fun to do this positive meditation twice over, thinking about the gender opposite to your own first, and then your own gender in a following self-therapy session. You will need four or five cards, as well as paper, crayons and a pen.

• Settle into a quiet space, and open the doors wide to your own creative imagination. Think about the gender that is not your own. Think about women (or men) in general, and maybe a few women in particular.

• As you think, begin to appreciate women (or men). Hold this willingness to appreciate in your mind and see what comes up.

As thoughts or images occur to you, put them down. No one will see this list but you. You can include idealised attributes and actual qualities.

Think about women (or men) in all kinds of situations: work, social, spiritual, emotional; on buses, on the sportsfield, changing car tyres; in bed; in the kitchen; as children, as adults; beginning life, ending life.

- When you have run out of aspects to appreciate, underline four or five qualities you appreciate most.

Write those qualities on the cards, one quality per card. Decorate the cards so you will enjoy looking at them.

These are qualities you can bring into your life. Your life need not be restricted to qualities associated with your own gender. As an adult, you can choose qualities from the whole range of human behaviour.

- Keep the cards prominently displayed. Return your awareness to them often until you feel those qualities are wholly yours.

Next time, do this active meditation thinking about qualities you associate with your own gender which are not as well developed in your life as they could be.

Use the cards. Use your awareness. Choose to have those qualities for yourself.

Silence is golden

Do you use too many words? In the babble of words between and around people there can often be little space for other more subtle and perhaps more truthful ways of communicating.

Women and men relating to each other often use words to devastating effect. Not only are too many words used, they are often virtually unintelligible to the other person.

I speak; *you hear me say something else.*

You speak; *I hear you say something else.*

I respond to what I believe you have said. *You become angry or discouraged.*

You respond to what you believe I have said. *I am furious that you are so insensitive to what I am sharing.*

Spending time with another person, without words, can be richly rewarding. First there may be embarrassment or awkwardness because the situation seems so contrived. Be patient, and willing to be a little creative in that silence.

Without words, you are forced back into your inner world.

Without words, you must draw on your own inner resources.

Without words, you have less defence against deep feelings.

• Spend time thinking and writing about the ways you feel about silence—and words. Visualise yourself in various situations and watch yourself as an observer might. Is there anything you want to change?

• Discover when you speak to

—Fill the space between yourself and others.

—Fulfil a social obligation.

—Defend against your feelings of emptiness.

—Prove you have something to say.

—Make yourself more dazzling than less verbal people.

—Protect yourself from entering the realm of feelings.

• Take time to note your experiences in your journal and to discover if you are using words to serve your deepest experience of self or allowing yourself to be used by words.

• After that session, try sitting for an agreed time (fifteen or twenty minutes) in silence with someone you care about. You need not maintain eye contact, but be together during this time and don't distract yourselves with reading or music. Hold your awareness that you are communicating with each other and inside your own selves—in silence.

After the agreed time is over, resist the temptation to burst into words to explain what your experience was like! There are other ways of sharing. Each person drawing an image of the experience to share with the other may be enough; or taking turns massaging; or making love when that seems appropriate to both.

• Notice what you were aware of when there were no words. Is that a quality or experience you would like to repeat, or explore further?

Your body is an expression of self

The ease with which you are at home in your body can colour how you accept the physicality of other human beings. It is, of course, possible to be easy-going with your body and still to be shut off from your feelings or so lost in your own feelings that other people's feelings scarcely matter. But it is also limiting to be locked into patterns of anxiety which limit your aliveness to your head only.

Accepting and loving your body is not narcissistic. For any of us, a loving relationship to our own body is a prelude to psychological and physical good health.

• Take your time to relax and enter a mood of pleasurable discovery. When you are ready, go inside—eyes closed, mind open and easy—to find an image for the way you feel about your body.

Draw the image, and use it as a starting point to explore beyond your familiar attitudes to your body.

• Looking at the image you have drawn, check for any tension that may exist between the way your body is, and the way you think your body ought to be (in order that . . .?). Write down what you discover.

Ask the image what it can tell you about your body's needs.

• Take time to appreciate what is precious and alive about your body, no matter how far from 'ideal' your body shape may be.

Write down any positive associations, no matter how tentative.

• Now bring to mind what you long for other people to appreciate about you.

Take time to appreciate that yourself.

Anchor your insight by writing that appreciation in your journal. 'I appreciate the strength in my legs. I appreciate the warmth of my smile.'

• Bring to mind what you long for other people to console you for.

Take time to console yourself.

Again, anchor your insight by writing. 'I understand my wish

to have fewer aches and pains.' 'I am sorry I can no longer move quickly.'
• Explore what treats you would like to give your body (a massage, a long walk, new clothes, delicious food, a lazy day).

Resolve to take time for those treats.

Listening to your body

Some people are easily and unselfconsciously tuned in to their bodies. If, like me, you live actively in your head and are less certain of what is happening from your neck down, this active meditation can help. (It is an adaptation of a routine that the Indian teacher, Krishnamurti, used and wrote about.) Practise it in a self-therapy session. Then you can adopt your own quick version and make it part of your regular early-morning routine. The goal is to open the information channels between mind and body.
• On waking, ask your body, 'How are you this morning?'

Move your awareness slowly around different parts: How are you, shoulders . . . arms . . . wrists . . . fingers? How are you, back . . . spine . . . .buttocks . . . belly . . . genitals?

Listen to what your body is 'saying' or what it is asking for.

Perhaps you want to get up and stand before asking, How are you, feet . . . calves . . . legs . . . thighs . . .? and so on, down to the ends of your toes, and round to the soles of your feet.

You may feel self-conscious initially, for do sensible people really ask, 'How are you, toes?' But take that silliness as an extra bonus, as gradually you will come to have a clear sense of what your body's needs are, whether for stretching, caressing or massage; for a brisk walk, a little more rest; for light foods, heavy foods; for affection or specific consideration.

'My body is worthy of my love'

Rewrite this affirmation in any way that inspires you. Continue to change it as your relationship to your body also changes. Each time you say it, check out the truth and depth of what you are saying. Where your words ring hollow, give that aspect special attention.

My body is worthy of my love.
My body is an expression of my unique self.
My body expresses my gender.
My body can express my sexuality.
My body is worthy of my pride.
My body gives me pleasure.
My body gives others pleasure.
My body is worthy of my tender understanding.
My body is worthy of cleanliness.
My body is worthy of good health.
My body is worthy of nourishing food and drink.
My body is worthy of loving touch.
My body is worthy of clothes that please me.
My body is worth listening to.
My body is worthy of my love.

Quaker listening

If this works for you, be grateful to George Sweet! He is a New Zealand psychotherapist who offers Quaker listening as a defuser in potentially tense situations. It is very simple.

Someone speaks.

You listen.

You use your awareness that what the person is saying describes their own experience. He or she is speaking out of their own experience — not yours.

You choose not to react. You do not argue. You do not engage.

You acknowledge what is happening only to yourself, 'There is Martha, going on again about her wonderful child's brilliant achievements . . .'

Freed from the need to react, to put right, to argue, to insist, you can let the moment pass by.

What a perfect way to conserve energy.

Dependence/independence

Sorry! There are many words to the exploration which follows. You may want to do no more than read them, plant a few seeds in your mind, and not return to the intensive exploration for weeks or months. This is a thorny issue for most of us, and eventually it will be worth taking the time to explore it because while you are likely to depend on other people for all sorts of things—love, accept-ance, affirmation, fun, sex, work, stimulation, inspiration, conso-lation—dependence is often experienced as though it were something to avoid.

It is as important to recognise and feel comfortable with your feelings of dependence as it is to be capable of independence. This is because the person who fears expressing any dependency needs is likely to feel cut off, undernourished, and unable to nourish others. Equally, it is empowering to know that some of your needs can be taken care of by your own self, or perhaps by a wider circle of 'others' than you may thus far have imagined.

Your relationship to dependence (and independence) can be explored over several self-therapy sessions, using self-questioning, drawing, your Magic Wand, and writing as your tools for discovery.

• Settle in to some embracing silence, taking time to relax your body and experience a feeling of openness and readiness. Now draw an image for what dependence means to you.

• Without stopping to analyse that first drawing, draw an image for what independence means to you.

• Using the two drawings as your starting point, spend time musing on those twin concepts, dependence and independence, separately first and then later in their relationship to each other, remembering that feelings of dependence, and acts of independence, are often a reaction to something from the past or to conscious or unconscious signals in the present.

Jot down single words as well as any phrases or sentences that occur to you as you look at your drawings, withdraw, reflect, write; withdraw, reflect, write.

If you feel stuck, think about what is going on right now in your life in relation to those twin issues: dependence and independence. Keep the associations close to home.

You can also hold the images you have drawn in your mind and use your Magic Wand (see p 28) to see if they have something to tell you.

If you are still stuck, take a few minutes to recall a recent situation when you experienced your independence or your dependence uncomfortably. Write about that incident in the present tense to keep it vivid ('Vinnie is telling me to take the car and get going . . .').

With this memory freshly recalled, return to your images and ask them again what they have come to tell you.

It is possible to take your exploration further.
• Using two (or more) large sheets of paper, list your positive associations with dependence and independence.
• Underline two or three words or phrases which seem to be the key ones. Now take time to reflect and ask yourself how those associations came to be positive: because that's what you were taught? Because that's what everyone thinks? Because those are your individual experiences?
• Having newly considered those positive associations, would you want to make any shift in your attitudes? If so, note that shift in your journal. You may even see a practical outcome of this shift. Note that too. ('I will allow other people to help me when my arthritis is bad. My independence need not be threatened by that.')

• Now list your negative associations with both independence and dependence.

Underline two or three words or phrases that seem particularly important. What is their history?

What did your parents teach you about dependence and independence through the ways that they lived their own emotional lives? Jot down your associations.

Where old injunctions are ringing in your head (*Stand on your own two feet. Don't you know when you are well off? I never had the time to feel sorry for myself.*), listen to those voices. Decide which messages have run their course. Formulate that awareness into a sentence or two and write it out in your journal ('I can accept help while standing perfectly well on both feet.').

• It is easy to use dependence or independence as a shield against self-awareness and growth ('There's nothing useful anyone else can tell me about myself . . .'). If that seems true for you, are you ready to let more complex insights emerge ('I'm willing to relax my old views and wait to see what emerges to take their place.')?

• Perhaps your feelings about dependence and independence are shaped by the way you feel about gender (Men are never dependent. Women always cling.). Returning to Women should/men should (see p 96) would support a change of attitude in the present.

Sometimes people fear dependency as a potential loss of self, or of autonomy ('If I depend or need a little, it will open up the floodgates.'). That isn't so. It is possible to be dependent *and* still to know where your boundaries are in relation to others.

• See yourself, in your imagination
—Expressing your dependence (or your neediness).
—Taking what the other person has to give.
—Feeling pleased by it, satisfied by it, *and still remaining intact*.
Holding onto positive experiences (see p 52) is a wonderful support if this last feels painful or impossible.

• Take time to formulate a modest, practical resolve, relating to a particular person or situation, where you will try a different expression of dependence and/or independence. Write your resolve in your journal.

If too little or too much dependence emerges as a problem for you, it is useful to check out if your dependency needs are spread beyond a single relationship.

• List your supports, reflecting on each area of your life in turn.

Are you able to acknowledge and develop those supports?

Are you able to acknowledge and develop the support you give others?

• Note in your journal any fear or resistance you may have when thinking about developing your capacity to be dependent (or independent).

If there are areas of your life where you are rigidly independent, are you ready to loosen up a little and take what others can give?

• Recall an actual situation when you allowed others to help or support you and that felt fine. Write a few lines in your journal about that situation.

Are there any insights from that experience you can apply more generally?

• Recall a situation when you were confident you were feeling or acting independently, and that felt appropriate and comfortable.

Again, what insights can you take from that situation to apply more generally in your life?

• If there are areas of your life where your dependency needs seem excessive, can you now see how some of those needs could be cared for differently: by you, or by a wider range of other people?

Formulate that resolve in a sentence or two, and write it in your journal.

If, after several sessions, this remains a painful issue for you, ask your Wise Being (see p 23) for some insight that will allow you to relax a little on the dependency issue. When Jutte did this, her Wise Woman gave her an image of a deck chair! Jutte imagined herself sprawling in this deck chair from time to time, detached from her usual responsibilities, taking what others were willing to give her. Then, as a deck chair is light and portable, she imagined also being able to fold it up, store it away, then bring it out again when the occasion seemed to call for it.

Using this image, Jutte was able to see that being dependent sometimes did not mean that she was becoming a dependent or weak person, but rather that she was growing in her capacity to take, as well as to give.

What matters in your life?

Your attempts to balance the different elements of your life—sex-love relationships with friendships; being a parent with being adult-child to your parents; paid work with leisure interests, time for personal growth and a spiritual life—can seem overwhelming.

• Explore what matters in your life. Become clearer about your priorities *at this moment*. Maybe some things can drop away, leaving you less burdened.

Write a list of all major roles, activities or relationships that take your time (parent, worker, chauffeur, cleaner, worshipper, life-saver, support to aged parents, etc).

Choose seven that seem most important.

• Have ready seven large sheets of paper. On each sheet make a drawing that represents your feelings about one of those seven activities, roles or relationships—*and the way it relates to your self*.

The drawing should be of an image that arises from within when you think about that function or role, a representation or symbol of an inner attitude, rather than a drawing of you doing or being whatever it is.

• After you have finished the seven drawings, spread them on the floor around you. Crouch down with them. Let them draw you into their space. Allow plenty of time for them to talk to you (see p 31).

• When you are ready, note in your journal how difficult or easy it was to explore, through drawing, each particular expression of self.

What areas of your life feel rich, abundant, or weak and starved for self-love and self-direction?

Is there any energy or learning you need to take from one part of your life to give to another? (This can be extremely helpful. Don't leave it out!)

Are there any insights you want to note and resolve to work with?

• When you have looked at those images for a long time, separately and in relation to each other, explore your deepest priorities. Use Free Writing (see p 32) to do this, returning to your guiding sentence, 'What matters in my life . . .', whenever you falter.

After writing, you may want to compare what has come up in different stages of this exploration. Allow yourself to be surprised.

• Before your session ends, take a minute or two to note any practical resolve that comes to your mind. Write it out so it is easy to remember and monitor. ('I am going to give most time to the things I will care about on my deathbed. These are . . .' 'I am giving up doing housework at the weekends. I will spend my time with the kids, cooking and seeing friends.')

Who can you blame?

The older child, and mature adult, is able to accept that Bad Mother and Good Mother are, in fact, one and the same person, and can tolerate the implications of that knowledge. Tolerating that knowledge precedes the capacity to acknowledge in yourself your own goodness and 'badness'. That capacity saves you from having to project all your 'badness' outside yourself and onto other people.

Blaming others is something most of us do easily. For children, blaming others actually does have a legitimate function. It protects the child's emerging ego from the damage that self-blame may inflict, and while the gradual learning of self-responsibility is central to a child's psychological development, it can nevertheless be helpful for parents to bear in mind the healthy self-protection that lies behind the child's drive to blame others. As adults, we have less excuse for blaming others and much more reason to develop self-responsibility. Indeed, one of the primary tasks of psychological maturity is moving from a stance in which we blame others to freeing others from our blame even while we may continue to acknowledge and remain aware of wrongs done to us.

This powerful meditation can help free you from painful resentments. I suggest doing it at a snail's pace over several sessions. Meantime, call on the wisdom of your Wise Being (see p 23). The Meditations on love (see pp 219, 221) also offer fine support.

• Take time to settle in to a quiet mood of discovery. Calm your breathing. Tell yourself you are going to explore who you want to blame, and for what, not to arouse painful memories, but to set yourself free by acknowledging the truth of what has happened and moving on from it.

Write down in as much detail as you can your memories, thoughts, feelings and grudges. Do so without any concern for fairness or legitimacy or clarity of expression. When you feel blocked in the writing, or distressed, it will help to use a guiding sentence ('I blame my Dad for . . .') and to incorporate into your writing exactly what is going on right now ('I feel so stuck and blocked up I don't know what else to write but my back is aching and suddenly I can hear again the slamming of the door as you came in Dad and I don't want to write it down but you bastard that stink on your breath. Now my hand won't write what came next and I am looking out of the window and listening to the trucks outside the house and I can remember that Mum used to say Thank God when you finally went off in your horrible green car you loved so much more than you loved any of us and . . .').

Stop when you have written enough for any one session (and have spent at least half an hour thinking, remembering and writing), knowing that you can return to the theme as often as you want, until you are ready to leave it behind.

• Before you close the session, take time to acknowledge to yourself that you have brought up and faced painful memories, and that you will honour today's achievements by returning to them.

Keep what you have written, even if you have no desire ever to re-read it. Place the pages in a folder until the active meditation is completely finished for you.

• Returning to the theme in a later session, continue to write—or draw images—in the same kind of way until the day comes when you return to this active meditation and feel empty. There will seem nothing left to write and little will to continue. It is not that you have forgotten what happened to you, but the blaming energy has died down, perhaps replaced by sadness, acceptance or distance, as well as vital clarity as to why some situations are painful or difficult for you in your current, adult life. *That day may take a month to come, or many months*.

On that day, choose to take all the many pages on which you have written and get rid of them. You may want to burn them, page by page. You may want to shred them, tearing them into bits and tossing the pieces into moving water.

• As you burn or tear or shred or throw, say aloud (or sing or shout) as often as you wish:

I am free of blaming.

I am free of blaming.

I am free of blaming.

• Be conscious of that freedom, and thankful for it.

Return to that feeling whenever you need to.

I am free of blaming.

The blamer and the blamed

Here is another way to ease the intensity with which you will be tied to someone else, as long as you are laying blame for the way your life is, or for the way you feel about yourself.

• Hold an image of the person you are blaming in your mind.

As you watch that image in your mind's eye, ask your Wise Being (see p 23) to let you know what was (or is) missing from that person's life. Be patient. Hold the image steady, without any particular expectation.

Eventually, and perhaps unexpectedly, you will have your answer. Write it down.

'Mum was incapable of showing warmth.'

'I realise Jack was missing the capacity to see his own mistakes.'

'Jennifer never learned to be anything but a flirt.'

'Eric had no insights about his gambling addiction.'

Incorporating your awareness of what that person was missing in their life may be part of understanding them. Understanding is not the same as forgiveness, and forgiveness may seem premature. However, accepting that the person was acting against your interests in part out of helplessness, or hopelessness, or grief, or anxiety, or incompetence, may give you a fuller picture of their human condition.

You may find it helpful now to breathe in peace and breathe out love, surrounding yourself with love, visualising this as a golden, healing light (see p 206).

Move on to the second part of this meditation only when you feel ready.

• Now you have some sense of what was missing in that person's life, ask yourself if those missing qualities are present in your own (the capacity to be generous, the strength not to be cruel, a freedom from a limiting addiction).

Where those qualities are present, bring that thought to consciousness. *Be grateful for your awareness of what you have.*

• Perhaps what was missing in that person's life is missing in your life also. This is not the time to blame yourself. See it as a chance to bring that quality into your life, or to be open to it coming into your life (see pp 62, 145, 146).

Again, end by breathing in peace, breathing out love.

Being ignored: an unexpected bonus

For women, encouraged to be aware of the needs of others, perhaps the most difficult juggling act of all is to find a balance between giving to others while still maintaining and honouring your own sense of self.

Your daughter tells you everything you think and say is boring.

Your husband reads his paper and grunts when you need to talk.

You look around for your son. His shoes and clothes and games and books are all over his room, but he is not.

Your aged parent dribbles, smells and calls you by your sister's name.

Your best friend tells you about her wonderful new friend with whom she will tramp in the Andes.

Your former school friend passes you in the street as your mouth begins to form a smile.

Your boss closes his door when he is in the most vital and interesting meetings.

• Take a break.

In the absence of their attention on you, you have a chance to

—Redefine your limits.

—Relocate your centre.

—Rediscover your self.

• It may take many months, or an hour, or minutes. What can help?

—A time of silence in order to relish a special memory.

—Appreciating a flower, drinking in its delicacy and perfume.

—A walk in a place and at a time of your own choosing.

—Listening to a favourite piece of music, sitting quietly or dancing as you do so.

—Taking a long bath, with scented oil added to the water.

—Hugging a friend and telling her how glad you are she is in your life.

—Enjoying time easily learning Yoga Nidra meditation (see p 265).

—Thinking creatively (see p 58) about *what being ignored allows*.

Affirmation for forgiveness

The capacity to forgive saves you from being tied to the past and allows you to be more alive and flexible in the present. Are you carrying a hurt from the past you now feel ready to let go? This does not mean you forget it. It means only that you are no longer gripped by it.

• Settle yourself into a quiet mood of discovery and reflection. Take a few minutes to recall the memory or image of the person you find it difficult to forgive. Recall how you must have felt at that time you were hurt, and acknowledge what murderous rage or bitter hurt you have felt since.

Take your time with this. Observe your thoughts and feelings as they arise, then, if you feel ready, let those thoughts and feelings pass from your mind.

• Acknowledge that you are ready to think about that person or event differently now: *not to remember it differently, but to experience its effects differently*.

Perhaps your inner world has an image to help you understand or put a distance between the pain you felt in the past, and the readiness to forgive you feel today. Take time to close your eyes and ask your inner world for such an image, then draw that image and experience what it wants to tell you.

Perhaps your inner world has a word you need, or a phrase. 'Elastic band' was what came to Gillian. She liked not only the flexibility that suggested, but also its circular shape which embraced a whole range of emotions.

• When you feel confident that you have traced your journey from anger and hurt to (relative?) forgiveness, try writing or speaking aloud the following affirmation. Rewrite it first in any way that seems appropriate.

Those who hurt me, I can forgive.

Those who offend me, I can forgive.

Those who ignore me, I can forgive.

Those who show contempt for me, I can forgive.

Those who fail me, I can forgive.

Those who cannot give me what I want, I can forgive.
Freer of resentment, I can create my life.
Freer of anger, I am open to be loving.
Freer of self-pity, I am open to my power.
Freer of burdens from the past, I can be fully alive in the present.
I choose the freedom of forgiveness.

• Continue to acknowledge mixed feelings as they arise. Write them down, tell them you are aware of them, but do not want to be overwhelmed by them. Return to this affirmation.

Loss and grief

In *Intimacy and Solitude* I wrote about the fear the infant feels when his (or her) mother abandons him, even for the few seconds or minutes it might take her to undo her clothes before putting her baby to the breast. As we become children, then adults, our capacity to tolerate an increasing degree of frustration grows. We learn also to tolerate our loved ones acting in ways which don't please us, as long as that's part of an overall loving, accepting picture.

However, in our body-mind that infantile longing for a haven of safety does not entirely disappear. As adults we will almost inevitably transfer that longing onto our most intimate relationships.

When we lose a primary relationship against our wishes, our howls of grief and rage arise from the depths of our being. We are living our pain in the present, and reliving our fear and pain from the past. This does not mean we are infantile or childish. It simply means that with the shock of the new, the pain of the old is reawakened. As we grew, our capacity to feel with our whole body-mind, as we did in infancy, had faded. *We had forgotten that it was possible to feel that bad.*

Being left—through death, a personality-changing illness or a unilateral separation—throws even the most emotionally resilient person back to a state of powerlessness which can feel intolerable. At such times your resources may seem almost to mock you in their inadequacy. It is only later, when the first waves of rage and grief have quietened down, that the foundations of your life can again be felt beneath your feet.

At times of powerlessness and loss, real live contact is needed with people who can bear to hear you speak out your pain. Lots of talking, crying, being unreasonable is completely legitimate here, lots of roaring like a lion or like the reawakened infant who is alive in your pain.

Grief counsellors, marriage guidance counsellors, telephone counselling services can all potentially be helpful. The following active meditation can help too. It acknowledges how you can be both a grieving adult and a frightened child. Read through the instructions before you begin, or record them on a tape with long pauses and time for reflection.

• Settle yourself comfortably. Slow your breathing. Centre your awareness. Bring to mind an image of the Eternal Mother, however she may appear to you. (This may be another name for your familiar Wise Being.)

• When you have seen and greeted in your mind the Eternal Mother, ask her to hold the frightened infant you once were. Ask her to rock the infant, cradle her, nurture her (or him) back to peace and calm.

You can envisage handing over your infant-self. Perhaps you want to watch as she nourishes that self? Or you may enjoy the feeling that you have entrusted the care of your infant within to the Eternal Mother, and can walk away.

Take all the nourishing you need. Take as much time as you need. Know you can return whenever you wish.

Rather than handing over an image of your infant self, you may want to see your adult self as small enough to be held, rocked, cradled, comforted. Anything is possible with the power of your imagination.

• As you observe your tiny adult-self in the arms of the Eternal Mother, take in all the consolation you long for.

It may help to rock as you sit, eyes closed. You are likely to feel sadness as well as relief. You may want to cry. Tears cleanse and heal. Let them come.

Only when you are ready, and when you feel that the Eternal Mother is fading from your mind's eye, bring yourself back to the present.

• Now promise yourself, and your infant within, that you will return often for love and consolation, and affirm that you are worthy of this care.

PART THREE

Solitude

'What would the shape of our aloneness look like if
we questioned it from the perspective of delight
instead of pain? {It} would look and feel like
uniqueness, a perspective of amazing richness that
no else quite duplicates; it would also look like
responsibility to give some kind of form to this
uniqueness; it would look like a basis for the
enjoyment *of other human beings.*'

Margaret R. Miles, 'The Courage To Be Alone—
In and Out of Marriage'

Introduction

Your capacity for solitude, for feeling comfortable when alone with your own self, exists on a continuum with your capacity for intimacy—being in good contact with others. This does not mean that solitude is a substitute for intimacy: it is a different experience of your same self ... It is, or can be, a unique source of joy, knowledge, ease and strength.

Working alone in self-therapy sessions, you are ideally placed to learn how nourishing your own company can be; what a packed, infinite storehouse you have of memories, dreams, desires, images and creativity.

Enjoying time alone; doing 'nothing' except drifting and dreaming; exploring and developing an inner life, becoming ever more aware of who you are and what your purpose is: these are pursuits given little value in contemporary life. Yet they are vital to emotional well-being, as is the capacity to explore and to know your moods, to escape the feeling that you are a victim of your moods, or helpless in the face of mood changes, by understanding that your 'moods' are a useful barometer of what is happening within—but need not be 'acted out' in old, unhelpful ways.

If, initially, you were to spend no other time alone except in your self-therapy sessions, and if you were to use your self-therapy sessions for nothing more than taking pleasure in your own company, then you would already have a new experience of solitude. And if being alone is already a vital or even a preferred way of being for you, then it may be that through persisting with your self-therapy, it can become a little less of a refuge and a little more a place of choice. Because in the ideal world we would move freely between intimacy and solitude, confident that each was continually available to us as a source of 'joy, knowledge, ease and strength'.

In the midst of life, with all its many and often conflicting demands, it is possible to develop a love for solitude and for quiet surrender to the moment-that-is. The rewards of that special kind of surrender are most tenderly expressed in the following lines. They were brought to my attention by my Quaker Friend, Shelagh Garland, and I thank her for them.

Enter into the stillness
inside your busy life.
Become familiar with her ways.
Grow to love her feel with all your heart
and you will come to hear her silent music
and become one with Love's silent song,
the Song of Songs.

Noël Davis,
'One with Love's Silent Song'

Understanding yourself and solitude

Solitude is a state in which, as Winnicott wrote, it is possible to be 'calm, restful, relaxed and feeling one with people and things when no excitement is around' ... If you can experience solitude rather than loneliness you have this capacity not because you possess a superior emotional backbone but because you have had satisfying connections with others. You have experienced, to re-use Winnicott's vital insight, 'being alone while someone else is present'.

To understand how you feel about solitude, you need first to explore your feelings about connection ('having' someone in a way that satisfies and sustains you). This exploration will take at least three self-therapy sessions and will benefit from return visits.

Approach each stage free of anticipation of any particular outcome.

• Make yourself comfortable, and prepare to welcome new insights. When your body is relaxed, and your breathing is steady and easy, turn on a light inside your mind so you can see thoughts and recover memories which have previously lurked in the dark.

• Start by thinking about what connection means to you. Write the word on a piece of paper, as often as you want: CONNECTION. When your thoughts and feelings begin to stir, write them down, focusing on the present. If an image rather than words occurs to you, draw it without analysing it.

• As you write or draw it may help to

—Visualise yourself connected (in physical proximity; through trust, distress, need, love).

—Visualise yourself connected to you in the same diverse ways.

—Bring your Magic Wand (see p 28) to your aid, letting it hover on the word CONNECTION.

• When you have fully explored what connection means to you in the present, thank your consciousness for what you have discovered, then cast your mind back to when you were twenty-one and repeat the process, seeing yourself in your mind's eye as you were then, and repeating your processes of discovery.

• Continue to move back in seven-year cycles until you reach the earliest months of your life. As an infant, you were incapable of thinking rationally, but you could experience with immense sensitivity what was going on in the world around you and how this reverberated within.

Ask your Wise Being (see p 23) for a symbol of this earliest experience of connection, an image to help you understand whether connection felt safe or unsafe for you. Was it something you could rely on, or something that felt precarious and scary? Accept whatever image arises.

Draw the image. Ask it what it can tell you, what it needs, what it wants from the adult-you, what it can give to the adult-you.

Write down whatever insights you gain.

At your next self-therapy session, repeat this active meditation, but this time explore your associations with SOLITUDE rather than connection.

Explore your associations in the present, and then in the past. When you reach infancy, remind yourself of Winnicott's phrase: 'being alone while someone else is present'. Be attentive to any associations that arise. These may be verbal, but be open to symbolic images also. Draw them or write them down without feeling the need to analyse them immediately.

In a third session, bring together the images you have drawn for connection and for solitude. Put them side by side so they can 'speak' to each other. Read through any words you have written. Allow their subtle meaning to reach you. Allow their related meanings to reach you. ('What can you tell me? What am I ready to know?')

Gradually allow those memories and images to let you discover *how your experiences of connection in the past affect your experience of solitude in the present.*

- Allow yourself to understand
—The ease or difficulty with which you 'take in' people, and 'carry inside you' your experiences of them.
—How this affects your willingness or unwillingness to be alone.
—That nourishing and nurturing yourself can make solitude as well as intimacy easier.
- Formulate any practical resolution that arises into a sentence you can write in your journal and monitor in a positive, self-loving way.

Affirmation while being alone

As with all the affirmations, rewrite this in any way you choose to reflect your own life, circumstances and feelings.

It may be useful to work with this affirmation first at a time when you are delighting in your aloneness. Then, when you have a bleak patch and feel lonely rather than alone, you can recall the affirmation *and* the positive feelings that first accompanied it. This will remind you that being alone can be positive, and that nothing stays quite the same—bad or good.

I am alone. *I am alone with my memories*.

I am alone. *I am alone with my thoughts*.

I am alone. *I am alone with my feelings*.

I am alone. *I am alone with my body*.

I am alone. *I am alone with my desires*.

I am alone. *I am alone with my plans*.

I am alone. *I am alone with my humour*.

I am alone. *I am alone with my Wise Being*.

I am alone. *I am alone with my capacity to make change*.

Your self in what is around you

It is possible to think of yourself as part of the universe, *or to think of the universe as part of you*.

I find this latter notion exhilarating and convincing, and most subtly helpful in times of loneliness. Here is a meditation which will allow you to experience 'the universe as part of you', but before you begin it you may want to read or even copy out two quotes which bring that idea to life.

'The Hopi tradition speaks of a fall from grace in which human beings experience themselves as progressively more separate from earth, animals and other humans. The return to grace is through reunion. The cause of the fall is ascribed to people's forgetting their true nature and purpose.'

F. Waters, *The Book of the Hopi*

'A unified world is a prerequisite for intuition . . . *the knower becomes one with the known, rather than observing it.*'

Arthur J. Deikman, *The Observing Self*

• Choose something in nature you find beautiful: a flower, a tree, a blade of grass, a cloud.

• Direct your consciousness outward. Go towards your flower or tree. *Enter the flower or tree.* When your attention wavers, or comes back to yourself, direct it outwards once more. The more frequently you do this active meditation the longer you will be able to stay 'out' and the more refreshing it will be.

• When you have been 'out' for long enough, bring your awareness back to your body, repeating these words aloud: 'In my body, in my body, in my body.' You may want to shake your hands and feet, or even your whole physical self.

• Later, write or draw about your experience, or simply send a flash of gratitude to the flower or tree or grass for receiving you so easily.

Your own most constant lover

In solitude you are aware of being alive and having needs, and of being able to meet some of those needs without turning to others. In solitude you do not feel empty. In solitude you do not fear death by emotional starvation.

The only person with you from birth to death is yourself. *Are you in loving company?* Increasing your self-love will not make you self-absorbed. It will make you less dependent and more available to others and *increasingly lovable*.

Here is a way to nurture self-love. Begin in a self-therapy session (thinking about self-love, writing, drawing) but extend beyond that initial session to a daily practice over several weeks—or a lifetime.

• Take two minutes to write a list of your shortcomings. Write as fast as you can—you're up against the clock. Now take the same time to write a list of your good points. Again, you are up against the clock. If the second list is shorter than the first, resolve to make this practice a top priority in your life!

• Make a note in your journal each day for at least a month of one thing you have done, said, thought or felt that day that the ideal lover would love you for, if she or he existed.

• Become aware of who or what the ideal lover would save you from. Give less energy to those people, situations or demands.

• Build up an awareness of what you like, admire, enjoy and *love* about yourself. *Consciously* give attention to that awareness. Write down what you appreciate in the most precise and detailed way possible.

• When you notice the usual din of self-defeating voices arising in your mind, mentally step back and disidentify from those thoughts.

Remind yourself: I have self-defeating thoughts. *I am not my self-defeating thoughts*.

• Know what you enjoy most about your own company. Spend time doing what you enjoy most: 'wasting' time, listening to radio plays, eating while reading, watching the TV shows of your own choice, taking long baths, taking pleasure in your body, making love to your body, praying, gardening, walking, meditating, dancing naked, playing brass band music, remembering your unique past, daydreaming about your future.

• If there are special pleasures you long to give to a lover, give them to yourself. Small gifts, delicacies to eat or drink, perfumed candles, flowers: you can receive those pleasures too.

• Should you feel your energy for this practice beginning to wane, it will help to review 'In the eyes of my ideal lover I am . . .' (see p 218), or to see what image emerges when you take time for Living with the Rose (see p 46).

Learning to be alone

You hate being alone. You avoid it at all costs. Perhaps you are even afraid to be alone. All your associations with being alone are negative.

Now you can discover what being alone could mean (pleasure in your own company; freedom to be with others because you want to and not because you have to).

Take these changes slowly. You may spend weeks or months with this, perhaps interspersing it with other self-therapy meditations as you go.

• Write down whatever thoughts, feelings and resistances arise as you consider the idea that you can develop through your practice of self-therapy a stronger, safer sense of self.

Do you have an image for that self, or a shape or a colour that you can jot down or draw?

Take at least fifteen minutes to write, withdraw; withdraw and write as you consider what this idea might mean to you. (Initially it may mean very little.)

• Write down your thoughts, feelings and resistances about the idea that having a stronger sense of self will change your experience of what it means to be alone (not *without* someone else, but *with* your own self, your own memories, the richness of your inner world).

Take at least fifteen minutes in each session to review what this suggestion means to you, and how it might affect your interactions with other people.

• Meantime, resolve how you can practise being alone for just a few minutes at a time.

Notice—and review—the times you are virtually alone, without having previously noticed (on the bus, in the car, in the bath, in the toilet). Appreciate that you can be alone at those times and may even like it!

It may help you to be alone if you preface those times with a few moments' conscious awareness: 'I am alone with my own self. I am alone with my Wise Being. I am alone with my capacity to breathe slowly, and to calm my body.'

• Once being alone seems a little easier, turn your attention to the pleasure of your own company. Explore your own company.

Again, use Free Writing and have as your guiding sentence, 'What I like best about my own company is . . .'. Perhaps there will be only little things to say initially (I don't answer back! I like my own smells. I can't offend anyone.). Be thankful for whatever modest insights come.

Continue to add to that list of what you enjoy about your own company. It may help to make this a written list. Then, when you feel panicky about being alone, *consciously* remind yourself what benefits your own company gives you.

The courage to be lonely

'We need new types of leisure which allow for contemplation and meditation. To this end, man [and woman] needs the courage to be lonely.'

Victor Frankl, *The Will to Meaning*

Adults need to be willing to tolerate loss and separation. That is crucial to emotional maturity. Loneliness is part of that—but it can be difficult to accept.

• Use a specific recent situation when you felt painfully alone, abandoned or isolated to explore your feelings about loneliness. You may want to draw an image for the way you felt then (or now). Don't analyse the image, but trust you can ask it what it has to tell you about the specific fears you attach to loneliness.

Later you may want to return to the same situation in your mind, jotting down any thoughts and feelings that arise; withdrawing to remember; writing, withdrawing; writing. Take your time with this. Write down whatever comes up, however off-track it may seem.

• Now you may want to broaden your view, moving through all the negative ways in which loneliness is described and exploited in our society, associating those with your personal fears and anxieties. Again, write then withdraw to think; write and withdraw, until you feel you have written down all you can.

• Know what you dread most about loneliness. Identify that by sitting still with the question until you feel you have a satisfactory answer, and then face it by writing it out as a complete sentence: 'What I dread most about loneliness . . . is that it will last forever.' It is often much easier to accept a fear or dread when it is out in the open and acknowledged.

• Ask your Wise Being (see p 23) for an image to support you through periods of loneliness. It could be a talisman of some kind, a Cloak of Warmth, or a candle sending out a friendly, guiding light. When you have that image, draw it, or note it in your journal. Use the image freely—both in prospect (when you are thinking about being alone) and in actual times of aloneness. You may also want to remind yourself that when you are alone you can summon up the steady, loving gaze of your Wise Being to support you.

Accepting a crisis

One of the challenges of time alone is making real the knowledge that crisis is best overcome by acceptance, rather than by denial.

When facing a crisis, or in the midst of one, it can be painfully tempting to think only a major shift or change will do. In fact, working through a crisis in small stages is invariably more positive, not only because it is more realistic, but also because it will allow deeper issues to emerge.

• Identify what your crisis is. Write it out in no more than a couple of sentences. If you can get it down to one, so much the better as that in itself will be clarifying ('I want to leave my partner but am afraid of losing my home.').

• Now, if you can, identify what your next step could be. (A next step is not an ultimate goal.) Write down what that next step might be. ('I want the courage to discuss my ambivalence with my partner.') See if it feels right to you.

Perhaps your anxiety is so intense you can't identify a next step. Then take your dilemma about not having a 'next step' to your Wise Being (see p 23). Ask for an image or a word to help you to understand what is going on and what a productive next step could look like.

Work with that image or word, if you get one, allowing it to guide you. ('An expensive linen tablecloth suggested to me I'd be better off discussing this in a public place than at home.')

• If you don't find an image or word, continue to alert your unconscious of your need for insight and a helping hand. Before you go to sleep, suggest your inner world sends a dream to guide you on this specific issue. Be sure to have paper and pen handy so that you can write down your dream as soon as you wake up. However unlikely your first impressions of the dream are, it may contain the fragment of information you need.

When 'nothing' happens, it is also worth teasing out that particular nothing to discover its special quality (see p 35). It could be a resistant nothing, a sad nothing, an old-pain nothing; it cannot be a nothing-nothing! Identifying your particular nothing can help you understand the deeper meaning of your crisis ('It's a cold lonely nothing. A chilly nothing. I am terrified my life matters to no one.').

Acknowledging that there is a deeper meaning to almost every external crisis does not make it easier to solve, but it does make it understandable when 'sensible', externally imposed solutions feel intrusive and inappropriate.

What's troubling you?

You may feel out of sorts, irritable, short-tempered, anxious or depressed and take this so much for granted that you don't explore what is lying behind that lack of pleasure and trust in life. Here are several different ways to explore what might be troubling you.

1 Go inside yourself, eyes closed and ask your inner world for an image that symbolises or represents what is troubling you.

Draw this image. Talk to it. Ask it what it wants. Allow it to speak to you in the first person (see p 31).

Perhaps 'nothing' keeps recurring. Ask nothing for its shape, how it feels, what its colour is; sense what mood it radiates. Draw or write what you know about nothing—then talk to it some more. Inside 'nothing' is always a clue that will be valuable to work with.

2 Use Free Writing (see p 32), taking as your guiding sentence, 'What's really troubling me is . . .'.

After fifteen minutes writing (when you are desperate for fresh realisations!) take the same time to think about what you have discovered in a curious, non-judgemental way. Then decide if some small change would ease your situation. Note that change in your journal where you can monitor it.

3 If you have someone you can trust, ask them to listen without interruptions or comment (see p 196). Use the same guiding sentence to keep on track and return to this same sentence whenever you need to. After your agreed time for talking, note any insights or feelings you may have in your journal, and anchor those with a small resolution you can monitor.

4 Use your voice and your breath to get closer to the quality of what's troubling you.

LOUDLY: What is troubling me is . . .

VERY LOUDLY: What is troubling me is . . .

BIG BREATHS OUT—Whoosh: What is troubling me is . . .

ARMS OUT TO THE SIDE AND HOLLERING: What is troubling me is . . .

TINY VOICE: What is troubling me is . . .

WHISPER: What is troubling me is . . .

Write down your insights in your journal, and note any brief, practical resolution you can now make to ease your troubled self.

Facing the impossible

> 'It has now been proved that though repression may be crucial for a child, it should not necessarily be the fate of adults ... we can regain our hope, if our distress signals are finally heard.'
>
> Alice Miller, *Breaking Down the Wall of Silence*

When you have experienced something that is impossible to talk about because it is too painful it will affect the way you feel about yourself. It will also determine whether—or how—you allow other people to get close to you. Unravelling that pain may be a long process, best done gently and gradually, but a first step may be to bring it into the open air by writing about it.

• Write to your Wise Being (see p 23), that part of yourself that can face this pain with courage and calm and can draw wisdom from events which seem initially to defeat you.

• Write as though you were writing a letter, but make it easy for yourself. Choose a time when you know that you won't be interrupted. Remind yourself that there won't be anyone to judge what you are writing or how you are expressing it.

• Trust that when it is difficult to continue the writing, you will tell yourself you are up against the wall of your own pain and will keep going. On the other side of any pain or resistance you feel, is the possibility of deepened insights, as well as feelings of acceptance and relief. With that relief may come sadness, grief or anger. Acknowledging those feelings gives you a chance to accept them, rather than using energy fighting them off.

• Keeping going is made much easier when you write down what is happening in the present moment.

'This is the hardest part. I don't want to write this because now I am remembering how ...'

'It is not fair that I am feeling so stuck and angry. It is not fair. It is not fair.'

'Writing this crazy letter is making me even more upset ...'

• Each time you get stuck, return to your thoughts in the present and start again.

'What I don't want to put on paper is that what really happened was . . .'

• Sometimes it is possible to recall a painful memory only in very small stages. (This has been absolutely true for me, and for people I have worked with also.) At the end of the day's writing

— Acknowledge how difficult it was to take that first step.

— Know that you can return as often as you want to this process of discovery.

— Feel confident that gradual discoveries are easier to assimilate than more dramatic moments of revelation.

• You will be helped by From fear to love (see p 221). It is a simple meditation, easily learned and healing in its effects.

• Keep your letter somewhere safe, perhaps in a sealed envelope. Acknowledge the *reality* of your hurt and pain. That alone can be extraordinarily vitalising.

Letting someone go

Perhaps there is someone you want out of your life, or even out of your thoughts—someone you resent, or find domineering; or someone who has wronged you in some way.

You can choose to distance yourself by persistent repetition of a simple meditation. Try it first in your self-therapy session, preparing yourself by relaxing your body and opening up the doors of your imagination.

• Visualise the person in a small boat. She or he is quite happy to be there. There is no sense of punishment or banishment.

In your mind, use your strength to push this boat away from land, away from where you are standing.

Watch, in your imagination, as the boat moves further and further from you, and becomes smaller and smaller until it disappears over the horizon.

As you watch it go, you may want to say goodbye. You may

want to offer some word of forgiveness or understanding, or you may want to say that it is not possible yet for you to forgive the person, but nor do you wish them ill.

Experience that you are freeing the person from the bonds of your negative attention, *and thus freeing yourself*.

• Next time this person dominates your inner landscape, pop them into the same small boat and, with a great imaginative heave, send them sailing off on the ocean of life all over again.

Releasing negative thoughts

'What we are today comes from our thoughts of yesterday, and our present thoughts build our life of tomorrow: our life is the creation of our mind.'

From *The Dhammapada*, trans. Juan Mascaro

Who is thinking your thoughts? *You are.*

Who is choosing your thoughts? *You are.*

Who is affected most by your thoughts? *You are.*

When you are alone, your thoughts about people and about your life are free to rise without external interruption. It is useful to watch the quality of those thoughts, especially when they are repetitive. If their mood is dark, angry, bitter or accusatory, ask yourself who benefits, *for you do not*. I am not suggesting that you should deny your darker thoughts, but negative thoughts will drain your energy and your potential for self-love.

From the work done by Carl and Stephanie Simonton with cancer patients comes a suggestion about letting go of negative feelings towards others. They suggest holding an image of that person in your mind and *imagining something good happening to them*.

Perhaps you are too angry, too hurt; you want nothing good to happen to the person. But can that really help you? I doubt it, especially when you are as closely connected as this kind of repetitive thinking usually implies.

• Take time to consider, honestly, what or who you think about, and what energy accompanies those thoughts. Spend at least fifteen minutes musing and jotting down your thoughts.

• Where change is needed, resolve to shift your thinking. There are several ways to do this.

—Letting someone go (see p 138).

—Following the Simontons' suggestion given above.

—Going to the heart of the issue (see p 142).

—Allowing aware breathing to shift your focus ('Breathing in I calm my body. Breathing out I smile.'). Unwanted thoughts might persist. Don't push them away; don't berate yourself. Tell those thoughts you are taking care of the issues that fuel them, then let them pass as though on a screen which is increasingly far from you.

Fleeing the cage of obsessive thoughts

How frequently time alone is spoiled by the tediousness of our thoughts, returning us obsessively to the same point of distress. This may be the wrong someone has done us; the unfairness of the world in general or a situation in particular; the failings of our own selves. Sometimes it seems impossible to break the pattern of such thoughts whether they are self-blaming and self-loathing, or blaming and loathing of others. Then we may long for the relief of someone to 'take us out of ourselves', but such company is not always possible or even desirable.

It is possible to free yourself from repetitive patterns of thinking.

1 Dance yourself free

Some things are possible to do simultaneously, but it is virtually impossible to dance vigorously to loud, joyful music while also harbouring obsessive thoughts! This is an aspect of your self-therapy you can share with others.

2 Massage yourself free

Play some music you find soothing and beautiful.

You may want to record these instructions before you begin. Do so slowly, and with loving anticipation of the pleasure you can give and receive—yourself.

• Bring your awareness to yourself. Close your eyes slowly. Notice your breathing—in, out; notice where your body meets the floor or chair where you are sitting or standing; notice where there are any points of discomfort in your body and ease yourself into a more comfortable position.

When you feel ready to do so, by slow stages move your awareness around your body.

Imagine that invisible hands are massaging you, stroking you in just the way you like best. These magical hands are able to move both on the surface of your skin and, where you need it, inside your body also. Move your awareness in a clockwise fashion around your body, first outside and then, should you feel so inclined, inside also.

Linger for as long as you want at the small of your sore back, or at the aching point between your shoulders. Perhaps it is your heart that needs attention, or your spleen. Perhaps you feel clogged up physically as well as mentally. Imagine those tiny hands working their magic on your digestive tract, your alimentary canal—and only when you have had all the pleasure you want, shift your awareness to a place just outside your body where your aura is.

• Still moving in a clockwise direction, allow your awareness of being stroked, massaged, caressed, nurtured stay just a few centimetres from your physical body's edge.

• When you are ready, open your eyes and slowly bring your awareness back into the room, into the here-and-now.

This, too, has changed.

Going to the heart of the issue

Sometimes your thoughts are obsessive or persistent because there is a pressing issue which you feel unready or unable to address. You can try one of several approaches (or, over time, all three!).

1 Free Writing (see p 32) can break the circularity of your thoughts and take you to the heart of the issue. Your guiding sentence could be, 'Inside the cage of my thoughts I am feeling . . .' Persist for at least thirty minutes. Your own boredom will drive you through the wall of your resistances.

2 'Unravelling the wool' is a meditation that can also help. You may want to pre-record the simple instructions.

• Visualise your thoughts as a ball of wool. See that ball of wool. Give it a colour, a weight, a texture. Is it tightly bound, or loose? Are there knots in it? Is it going to be easy to unravel, or will you have to be patient? When you are ready, begin to unravel the ball of wool.

Continue to unravel the ball of wool in your imagination, and *see your thoughts unravelling with it*. When you come up against a problem in the unravelling—a knot, a lost end—deal with the problem slowly and with care. Enlist your creativity as an ally. Take your time. Know that when the ball of wool is fully unwound you will literally have unravelled your thoughts and the confusions that accompany them. It is all right to leave the pile of wool unwound. Place it, in your imagination, on an open dish or platter, where sunlight can fall on it, lighting it up.

Now you will become aware that sitting on the pile of your unravelled thoughts is an image for what is worrying you, or perhaps it is a word. Know you are ready to see that image or word. Take your time. Perhaps you understand the image or word at once. Perhaps the image is obscure or unexpected. That's fine. Whether or not you fully understand or can accept the image, trust that insight and clarity will follow.

• Take a few minutes to write about the experience, and any insights you drew from it.

Acknowledge the trust you feel that, when you are ready, you will receive any additional insight and clarity you are seeking.

3 If you have someone who can or will listen, ask that person to listen intimately (see p 196), limiting yourself to an agreed time.

After speaking, write in your journal how you felt as you spoke, how you feel now, and what insights you have gained.

Assure yourself that if there is a problem fuelling the chorus of voices in your head, *you have the resources to understand that problem.*

Just standing

Sometimes doing nothing serves us best. But for goal-directed Westerners that can be painfully hard to learn! Here is a famous Zen tale to help.

'Once there was a man standing on a high hill. Three travellers, passing in the distance, noticed him and began to argue about him. One said, "He has probably lost his favourite animal." Another said, "No, he is probably looking for his friend." The third said, "He is up there only to enjoy the fresh air."

'The three travellers could not agree and continued to argue right up to the moment when they arrived at the top of the hill.

'One of them asked, "Friend, standing on this hill have you not lost your favourite animal?"

'"No, I have not lost him."

'The other asked, "Have you not lost your friend?"

'"No. I have not lost my friend either."

'The third traveller asked, "Are you not here in order to enjoy the fresh air?"

'"No."

'"What then are you doing here, since you answer 'No' to all our questions?"

'The man on the hill replied, "I am just standing."'

Adapted from *The Gospel According to Zen*,
edited by Robert Sohl and Audrey Carr

The Mothergod who never withdraws

'In solitude our deepest intuitions of an indwelling personal God Spirit are confirmed, the Mothergod who never withdraws from us and whose presence is our existence and the life of all that is. Her unveiled glory is too great for us to behold; she hides her face. But we find her face in reflection, in sacred guises, mediated through the natural, elemental symbols. It is the response to them that matters, the desire to receive with animation those messages carried through our nervous senses and the will to focus their energy and transform it into worship.'

Meinrad Craighead, 'Immanent Mother'

• Draw or write what arises for you as you read these lines. Let them work on you and through you.
• Later, ask yourself whether there are fresh ways you could nourish your experience of an indwelling spirit, or open yourself up to the possibility of such experiences.

Perhaps your Wise Being (see p 23) has something to tell you.

Perhaps the beauty of nature, of music, of poetry, will allow you to connect from within to All-That-Is, or, as Meinrad Craighead chooses to call it, the Mothergod who never withdraws.

This is not a time for probing and analysing. Sitting, dreaming, waiting and perhaps receiving: that is part of self-therapy—and part of life. It may even be central to it; I suspect it is.

Talking to your moods

'I was in this foul mood,' people often say, as though the mood has, like a raincloud, descended upon them, rather than rising from within and expressing something from their inner world.

If you have moods that worry you—or anyone else—try this.
• Write a letter to your mood, addressing it as though it were a real entity: Dear Bad Temper; Dear Melancholy; Dear Listlessness . . .

When you feel you have nothing further to say, write, PS I just want to add . . .

• Then, when you have absolutely nothing else to say, shift your position so that you *face the place* where you have just been writing.

• Take a clean sheet of paper, settle into the moodiness of that mood, and imagine how your personified mood might reply. Write down whatever comes into your mind without censoring it or judging it. Allow the mood to tell you what it wants or needs, or is struggling to express.

• Now that you understand your mood a little better—and *how you can affect the mood*—be open to formulating a practical resolution that will allow you to get what you want (or what your mood wants) in a more positive way. Here is what Marianne discovered.

'I've always been sulky. I hate being called sulky but I've also accepted it. In my childhood I would sulk when my feelings were hurt and I had no comeback. My lover also accuses me of sulking. Whilst writing to my sulkiness I discovered that I am angry because she is articulate and when I am upset I feel lost for words. So, my sulkiness is a place to be safe without words. I'm not quite sure what my resolution is yet, but I will start by explaining to Chandra that her wordiness makes it harder for me to speak when I am upset. Then my sulkiness is like an old security blanket I need to snatch up and cuddle into. Maybe together we can work out a different way.'

Meditating on the quality you most desire (1)

This is a favourite psychosynthesis exercise and can be done with positive results by children as well as adults, though with children it may need to be emphasised that you are evoking positive qualities and not asking for material *things*, or the means to buy material things!

• Have a card and some crayons by your side. Take time to calm your mind with a few slow, relaxing breaths.

• Now allow a word to enter your mind which describes a quality you'd like to bring into your life. *This quality should be positive.* It might be trust, love, serenity, peace, faith, openness, co-operation, playfulness, mindfulness, simplicity.

• Write the word on a card in big letters. Decorate the card in whatever way suits your chosen word.

Place it in a room where your eyes will light upon it regularly through the day. Each time you see the card, bring that desired quality into your conscious awareness.

After a week or two, or when you feel ready, repeat the exercise. Soon you will have a constant supply of beautifully decorated cards supporting you as you bring more of the qualities you desire into your life.

Meditating on the quality you most desire (2)

This is another adaptation of a psychosynthesis exercise.

The quality I am currently meditating upon is serenity. I am, alas, not a good advertisement for the meditation, but nevertheless this practice brings immediate benefits. You can choose from any positive quality you would like to bring into your life. Substitute that quality wherever I use the word 'serenity'.

It may happen that when you slow down to think about a desired quality only negative thoughts come into your mind. Don't fight them off. Simply leave this active meditation and explore those more pressing feelings by writing or drawing them out (see pp 30, 32). You can return to the meditation later, and it may feel especially strengthening for you once your negative feelings have been acknowledged and accepted.

• Have to hand a pen or coloured pencils, and a large sheet of paper in the centre of which is written your seed word: SERENITY. Settle into a quiet space inside yourself. Take some deep breaths, letting go—for a short while—your concern with things outside yourself.

• Think about serenity (or your chosen positive quality). Hold the word in your mind and reflect on its nature, its meaning for you, and whatever images or associations you have with it.

When you are ready, jot down on the sheet of paper any associations you have with the word 'serenity'. These do not need to make any immediate sense.

• Return to the meditation. Go more deeply into the idea of serenity. Praise serenity in your mind. Welcome serenity. Desire it. Long for it. Reach out to it.

Jot down further associations, allowing them to radiate outwards from the word sitting in the centre of your page.

Spend at least fifteen minutes withdrawing, writing; withdrawing, writing.

• Assume a physical pose of serenity. Experience serenity throughout your being: in your mind, your feelings, your body. Be, for a moment, serenity. Express serenity on your face; in your breathing.

• Jot down any fresh associations with serenity which now come to mind.

• See yourself in a place which makes you feel serene: by the ocean, by a lake, in a quiet room. Repeat the word serenity slowly and with loving attention as you linger with that image.

Write again, if you want to.

• There may be a piece of music, a particular writer or a painting that you associate with the quality of serenity. When you have identified something to inspire you, resolve to spend time listening to that music, reading that writer's work or looking at that painting.

• Promise yourself that to the best of your ability you will be serene throughout your day. When you lose contact with serenity, trust you can return to it: serenity is there for you.

Compose a simple statement of intent and write that on your

serenity page, or in your journal. ('I will pay attention to the tension in my face, allowing it to relax into an expression of serenity at least on the hour and half hour.')

Your inner happenings

'My life has been singularly poor in outward happenings. I cannot tell much about them, for it would strike me as hollow and insubstantial; *I can understand myself only in the light of inner happenings*; it is these that make up the singularity of my life.' [my italics]

C. G. Jung, *Memories, Dreams and Reflections*

• Take time to note your inner happenings when you write in your journal: how you feel, what you long for, what delights you, what has made you sad, what is driving you forward, whether you feel in touch with others and yourself, how real and true to yourself you are feeling, or not.

• Use your awareness to build up an experience of an inner life that is as rich in happenings as your outer life.

• Learn to trust 'messages from the inside'—through dreams and active meditations—at least as much as advice from others.

• Explore how you can choose to think positively, to react generously, to give yourself as well as others the benefit of the doubt.

• Read what will enhance your inner life. Walking in beautiful surroundings, pausing to take in the beauty of a tree or flower or bird; listening to music, to children playing; touching another human being respectfully and with love; expressing care and kindness, thoughtfulness and joy: these all enhance your life within.

• Take time to be thankful.

Finding the joy in your day

'He [and she] who has no fear of life and can relate in love is much more likely to let go of life with acceptance and confidence.'

Lily Pincus, *Secrets in the Family*

Are you allowing yourself some moments of pleasure in life, and a small experience of love each day?

• No matter how far from perfect your day may be, end it by finding at least one moment for which you can be thankful.

Note that moment in your journal. Tune into it. Allow it to become your tune. Don't postpone your capacity to live.

• When you can find no moment which gave you joy, or for which you can be thankful, it can help to review your day *as though it had happened to someone else*. Run it backwards through your mind (starting from the evening and working back to morning). When you notice even a potential moment for joy, peacefulness or appreciation of or from another person—or any other positive quality—allow your Observing Self to point that out to your Learning Self ('See, that's when you could have allowed yourself to laugh!'; 'See, talking a few minutes longer with that neighbour could have been rewarding.'; 'In the park as you went to work, did you see that the gardens were full of spring blossoms?').

• Allow the Observing Self to be your guide. Look forward to what she/he has to teach you.

Continue this practice daily. It develops an attitude of mind, and does so quickly, until you are spoilt for choices of joy-filled or positive moments.

Pleasure and death

For most people the associations between death and solitariness remain largely unconscious and therefore easy to deny although not so easy to defend against. Such defences might be recognised as a whirl of activity which makes solitude unlikely and introspection 'impossible', or perhaps as depression, a partial death that is better than a total death.

Are you able to experience pleasure without also anticipating the end of pleasure?

Are you able to experience life without also anticipating the end of living?

Only when you can accept your own mortality do you have a chance to live life to the full. Yet so many of us avoid thoughts of death. We deny the 'little death' of our own isolation; we prefer depression or a half-life to the risks of experiencing our own deep feelings.

• Gently, and with respectful curiosity, ask your inner world for an image for the way you feel right now about pleasure. Draw that image quickly without censoring it or analysing it. Then take time to withdraw into yourself again and ask your inner world for an image for the way you feel, now, about death. Draw that image alongside the image for pleasure.

If you want to do more than see those images together, and let their meaning emerge slowly, you can ask each one if it has something to say to the other, or something to say to you. Write down whatever thoughts or associations come as answers. If the images are disturbing or distressing, ask them why they have come at this time, what they need, and what you need to understand from them. Approach them fearlessly. They have arisen from within you in order to increase your familiarity with what anyway exists in your own mind.

• Free Writing (see p 32) will help you explore your feelings further. You may want to choose your own guiding sentence this time, but these suggestions will get you started.

'I stop myself feeling pleasure when . . .'

'Thinking about the death of others I feel . . .'

'I will not be ready to die until . . .'

Take time at the end of writing to review what you have written and to note any insights that may have occurred.

• Make a brief, practical resolution to live *in the present*. When you are prevented from being in the present by your anxieties about past events or the future, don't chastise yourself, just make a mental shift into the present again. Note your progress in your journal.

After I am dead

This is not an active meditation to increase your morbidity! On the contrary, it will help you appreciate the precious gift of life. It would, however, be wise to do it when you are not feeling depressed or overcome with a sense of worthlessness.

Do you remember as a child feeling comforted by telling yourself that those people around you (who may have hurt you) would be 'sorry when I am dead'? It may be that you even elaborated the details of your dying, your death and the tears and regrets which would follow.

As an adult some of that feeling may be with you still: a suspicion that there are insights about you that others won't have until you are gone, or aspects of you that are not fully appreciated by others while they can still take you for granted.

Or maybe you are aware that should you be dead by tomorrow, there are aspects of other people you would regret not fully appreciating: things you might have said, efforts you might have acknowledged, hugs you might have given. The following meditation will explore this.

• Relax your mind, your body, knowing you are going to take time away from your usual concerns. Check that your body is comfortable. Where it needs to relax a little, give it the attention it needs.

• Now, slowly imagine that you are dying. This process of dying can be observed by you with relative detachment, almost as though it were happening to someone else. But it is not someone else; it is you. Because it is you, you know what you are thinking, feeling, desiring as you die. You know what you are regretting. You know what you are finding hard to let go. You are watching the faces and reading the hearts and mind of those who are witnessing your dying.

Take as much time as you need to see this process, and to gather from it all the information you need. As thoughts and feelings occur to you, write them down, then withdraw to consider this imagined scene several more times, writing as you continue to have insights.

Perhaps an image comes into your mind. Draw it without stopping to analyse it.

• Now shift your mind forward a little. You have died. Perhaps you have been dead for several weeks. You are now able to observe your life with the benefit of hindsight.

As you review your life, what do you become aware of? What was missing? What was left undone? What do you wish you had done differently? What can you feel happiest about, and get most satisfaction from? These are big questions. Take all the time you need for them.

Write down your thoughts and feelings, no matter how unexpected these may be. Withdraw to contemplate; write; withdraw, write.

• Now take a couple of big breaths—in, out, in out—and imagine that, completely unexpectedly, you have a second chance! Take time to appreciate this chance. Appreciate that your life is not yet over, that whatever remains undone could now be done. How does that feel?

Follow that feeling, and allow it to tell you what you have learned from your 'dying' and from your 'death'. What have those experiences highlighted, simplified or clarified?

Note in your journal any simple, practical resolutions you want to make in the face of this 'second chance'. Know you will feel their effects in your daily life. Formulate them as acts of will: 'I will give more time to . . .'; 'I will refuse to be distracted by . . .'; 'I will accept my responsibility for . . .'; 'I will open my heart to . . .'

• If it feels appropriate, spend a few moments in thankfulness: for the gift of life itself, for the awareness you have about your life, for your capacity to make choices.

Wanting nothing, getting everything

'I had found myself staring at a faded cyclamen and had happened to remember to say to myself, "I want nothing". Immediately I was so flooded with the crimson of the petals that I thought I had never known what colour was before.'

Marion Milner, *A Life of One's Own*

• Spend some time experimenting with the idea of letting go your expectations of how people or situations must be (to console you, gratify you, reassure you, limit you).

Start by imagining approaching a flower without any expectation of how it should smell or feel.

Now imagine approaching someone you know well, without any preconceptions: as though this were your first moment of meeting.

Now imagine entering a familiar situation, 'not knowing' what will follow.

Re-create being alone in your mind, free of past associations of what 'being alone' means to you. Imagine it as an entirely new experience you are eager to try.

• Write down what arises from those imaginative explorations. Note your resistances also! Many people dread 'not knowing'. Are you one of them? Marion Milner's phrase may help: '[I] happened to remember to say to myself, "I want nothing".'

• Review this capacity regularly. Do it imaginatively and in daily life, encouraging yourself to be mindful of what is happening *in the very moment of your awareness*.

• At the end of each session on this vitalising issue, anchor your insights with a modest, practical resolution, written in your journal. See it as a liberation of the most delightful kind.

PART FOUR

Intimacy

'How one conducts one's life, what one does in daily life—not at a moment of great crisis but actually every day—is of the highest importance. Relationship is life, and this relationship is a constant movement, a constant change ... In relationship alone can one observe oneself; there all the reactions, all the conditionings are exposed. So in relationship one becomes aware of the actual state of oneself.'

J. Krishnamurti, *You Are the World*

Introduction

We do not speak of ourselves, but as
we walk down the stairs snow falls,
coming to lay soft stars on the dark
tweed of our hearts. We brush away for
each other the little messages of death.

Lauris Edmond, 'Love Poem', *Selected Poems*

Self-therapy is the ideal safe space in which to explore a whole range of intimacy issues: to try out new ways of being and to review current patterns to see where they're not working well for you, and what could take their place.

In self-therapy, you tune in to your own reality as truthfully as you can, *and risk being changed by that experience.*

In situations of intimacy you tune into someone else's reality, *and risk being changed by that experience.*

Working on issues of intimacy in your self-therapy, you will find that your capacity for intimacy reflects your self-awareness, self-love and self-trust. Developing trust in your inner world, feeling freer to observe your own self-defeating behaviour without falling into the pits of self-hatred; feeling empowered to make positive changes: this will bring you closer to other people and will allow you to explore ways of being open and accepting to a whole range of intimate experiences, rather than seeing intimacy as something which happens between two people, between two sheets.

The comfort of human contact is something we all need. Loving and being loved; listening and being listened to; touching and being touched; laughing with, feeling special; appreciating and being appreciated: I want all of that, and I expect you do too.

This book cannot bring those experiences into your life, but by working with self-therapy you can develop some understanding of what is cutting you off from your longed-for experiences of intimacy. You may also discover that the needs you thought would never be met can be expressed in many different ways, for self-therapy develops your capacity to make a creative response to difficulties and to see opportunities where previously it seemed that none existed. It encourages mindfulness (awareness of what is). That, in turn, allows you to appreciate what you already have and nurture that, rather than longing for what may always be in the future.

Self-therapy encourages living truthfully, richly; inwardly as well as outwardly—and it certainly encourages intimacy: intimacy with your own self in times of solitude, and with others when that is appropriate. To live with an openness towards other people is the best possible expression of your awareness that you are making your way in a world filled with human beings who have longings, dreamings and desires close to your own.

Understanding yourself and intimacy

The freer you are from expectations of what intimacy is, the more likely it is that you will be open to enjoy what intimacy can be.

• Spend time exploring what the word INTIMACY means for you. Jot down single words or whole sentences quickly and freely, returning from time to time to hold the word INTIMACY in your mind, until new associations occur to you. These questions may help.

What are the qualities you associate with intimacy?

What is it about intimacy that rewards you?

What is it about intimacy that eludes you?

What are your inspirations for intimacy?

How do you expand your vision of what intimacy could mean?

Are there books, poems, paintings or music that would nourish your vision of intimacy?

• Make an achievable resolution to bring into your life more of the qualities you associate with intimacy. Note that resolution in your journal.

• Decide how you can bring those qualities into an ever-widening circle of relationships.

• Is your way of being in the world intimate (true to who you are; open to who the other is)? If not, what small, practical change needs to be made right now? Note that change in your journal.

• At any time when intimacy seems to 'fail' you, return to explore what needs and wants you are loading onto the idea of intimacy.

Check: can experiences between human beings carry such a burden?

Meditating on the self of the other

It is only too easy to get caught up in the behaviours and attitudes—or problems—of another person, and lose sight that they are, like you, a self.

You can record these instructions, or read them through before you start.

• Close your eyes. Shut out for a little while the world around you. Bring to mind an image of someone you care about, or are having difficulties with.

• Allow your usual thoughts, feelings and associations with that person to arise—and to pass by.

Gradually focus on the thought that this person is, like you, a self: whatever that term means to you in its embracing of all that we can know about a person, and all that is yet to be revealed.

Gently return to this idea of the other person as a self, whenever your attention wanders.

• You may want to ask your inner self for an image of that other person's inner self: hold that steady. Regard it with respect. It may give you a new depth of insight about that person, or fresh compassion.

• When you feel ready to do so, open your eyes.

Be thankful for any insights, however fragmentary.

If you to want to make a small change in behaviour or attitude towards that person, write it down as a single-sentence resolution in your journal.

Your idea of intimacy and mine

When two people are in a close relationship, not necessarily a sexual one, it can be illuminating to compare, lovingly and without criticism, the meaning each brings to the idea and the practice of intimacy. If both people are willing, each can do separately the two preceding active meditations and share what they have written and drawn in a spirit of discovery.

• Be aware of *how* you are listening to each other talk about your intimacy needs and expectations (see p 197). That can be part of understanding how you practice intimacy, as well as what you want from it.

• Where your partner's experience or expectations differ from your own, regard this as a way to expand your vision, rather than experiencing the difference as a criticism or potential problem. Differences are as much part of intimacy as similarities. It is important to honour that.

• Ending this exploration together, you could enjoy this beautiful exercise I have adapted from Lucy Goodison's *Moving Heaven and Earth*. Her version is called 'Using a Symbol with a Sexual Partner', but close friends or relatives who are not sexual could also do this together.

— Each choose a symbol for intimacy. (Go into yourself and ask your inner world for the symbol you need.) When you each have a symbol, talk about them *and find a way to combine them*. (My ring is threaded with your flower. Your rock pool harbours my tortoise.) Check out that you are both happy with the way your symbols hold each other, and combine.

— Now sit comfortably, facing your partner. Bring your attention to your partner's midriff area (solar plexus). Then bring your awareness to the space between your two bodies. See your combined symbol in that space between you. Sit in silence without touching for five to thirty minutes.

During the meditation the symbol may change for one of you. It is fine to talk about that, and how the exercise felt for each of you. Return to the exercise as often as you wish.

What matters to you more than intimacy?

Most of us would like to believe we give intimacy a high priority in our lives. This may not be as straightforward as we think!

• Use Free Writing (see p 32)—and a very open mind—to discover what matters more to you than intimacy. Take as your guiding sentence: 'More than intimacy I need . . .'

As you write the same sentence many times, review different aspects of your life: at home, at work, with close friends, colleagues, competitors. See yourself in repose. Remind yourself when you feel most alive. Check out what you give your time and energy to; where your ambitions are focused.

Here are some examples, painfully and sometimes slowly discovered by others: control, sexual freedom, looking good, money, peace and quiet, security, political activity, career success.

• Are the priorities you have discovered to your liking?

If not, make a conscious decision to give energy and consideration to what matters most to you at this time in your life.

Formulate that decision into a specific resolution and note it in your journal or on a large card that cannot fail to remind of your new-found priorities!

'I want love'

'To look for love is a totally unsatisfactory endeavour and will never be satisfying. It sometimes works and sometimes doesn't. That which does work is *to* love. This brings emotional independence and contentment. Loving others is possible not only when the other person is accepting it but at other times too. Loving others has nothing to do with them. Loving others is a quality of one's own heart.'

Ayya Khema, *Be An Island Unto Yourself*

When you want love and do not have it, or do not have it in the form you idealise, it is tempting to despair, rage, fall into self-blame, or to blame your parents, God or the universe.

It *is* possible to be aware of wanting love—and to avoid those painful cycles of self-hatred and blaming. It *is* possible to awaken yourself fully as a loving person.

Most of us tend to hope that this will bring us the love we want—perhaps in the shape and size, the age and income bracket we want! Yet if you can focus on developing your capacity to love, without expectations or desires for a particular outcome, then what you have perhaps been blind to thus far may reveal itself.

• Over the course of several weeks, take time each evening to note briefly in your journal the small ways in which love was expressed towards you that day, and how you were able to express love towards others. Love may not always be dressed in the robes of passion; it may be expressed as consideration, thoughtfulness, patience, tolerance, humour, appreciation.

When this seems difficult, Finding the joy in your day (see p 149) will support you.

• Be creative about ways to express yourself as a loving person.

Note in your journal any thoughts or resolutions you have.

• Be consciously thankful for any expressions of love which lighten your daily life. Returning to those moments in thankfulness anchors them, and allows you to enjoy them twice over.

Hungry for love

It is fine to be hungry or even greedy for love. We all need to love and to feel lovable, even when that's hard to admit. And it's good to know that you do not need to wait for someone else to prove that you are lovable. Indeed, your hunger will best be satisfied when you can develop *your capacity to be loving*.

The more you experience and exercise that capacity to love—to love life, God (if that seems appropriate to you), yourself, others, nature, poetry, ideas, music—the less anxiously you will need one single person to affirm you.

Start small.

• Think about the relationships that are in your life already, no matter how far from ideal they may be. It may help to list them. Include marginal relationships also (the people you see at the bus stop, at the school gate, colleagues at work).

• Now promise yourself you will bring to each of them a tiny extra percentage of loving. Resolve to increase that percentage each week or month.

Don't do it so you will be loved more. You may not be. *Do it to grow as a loving person.*

Loving doesn't mean being a slave to other people. It means being ready to accept them for their failings as well as their strengths; rejoicing in the ways they are different from you as well as similar; taking for granted they won't always behave as you want them to; assuming they will disappoint you sometimes—and that you can cope with that.

Loving is also taking pleasure with and in others: talking, laughing, affirming, sharing, listening, sitting in companionable silence, touching, hugging, restraining, honouring; sharing food, ideas, good and bad news; confiding deep feelings; accepting.

• Visualise how your relationships might be, and how you might feel, if there is that extra percentage of love circulating around them.

• Note your progress in your journal. While avoiding harsh self-judgements, observe what makes it harder or easier to increase your capacity to love. Use your self-therapy to gain any extra support you need.

'I am loving'

At any time of the day or night, but *often*, take some moments to bring your awareness to your heart (see p 240) and repeat the words 'I am loving'.

Sometimes you will want to say the words quietly. At other times you might want to sing, roar, shake your body or dance as you repeat this beautiful, powerful and eventually truthful phrase. As you say the words, move your awareness around your body:

I am loving in my toes.

I am loving in my ankles.

I am loving in my thighs . . . my calves . . . my groin . . . the small of my back . . . my belly . . . my breasts/chest . . . my spine

... my armpits ... my shoulders ... my arms ... my wrists ...
my fingers ... my thumbs ... my neck ... my throat ... my
tongue ... my face ... my ears ... my eyes ... my brow ... my
hair. And so on, round again.

You can move your awareness through your senses, and your
mind. You can add:

I am loving in my memories.

I am loving in my intentions.

I am loving in my laughter ...

• Sometimes you may want to write down the feelings that arise in
you during or after the meditation and pay them some attention.

Accept and give time to the grief or choked-up feelings that
might occasionally accompany this meditation, as well as the joy
and expansiveness you will also feel.

Unconditional love

Most of us give lip service to how splendid unconditional love is,
even while practising conditional love most of the time. Distinguishing between *who the person is* and *whether the person is acting
as we want them to* is a step towards the practice of unconditional
love. But even when we believe we are distinguishing between
being and acting, that won't carry much weight if our language,
gestures, our measures of acceptance all tell others that we can only
love them when ... only love them if ...

This meditation is revealing for many kinds of relationships and
can be especially useful for parents to do in relation to their
children. It will bring a fresh awareness of the extent to which your
affirmations and expressions of love are tied to the children fitting
in with your expectation of how they ought to be (so you can love
them—or preserve intact your picture of yourself as parent).

• Take seven pieces of card. Bring to mind someone who is
important to you. Holding that image of the person in your mind,
write on each card: 'I love you when ...'

• With all seven cards laid out in front of you, reflect on the extent to which your love *is in reaction to* what the person is doing, or failing to do.

How would you like to change that, if at all?

Note your insights, your mixed feelings, your resistances and any resolution you need to make in your journal.

• Decide how, over several weeks, you will monitor in your journal how conditional your expressions or feelings of love were during that particular day.

• Decide, too, how you will allow yourself to be unconditionally *self*-loving.

Your capacity to love others reflects your capacity to love yourself. Increasing self-love will bring you closer to others; in turn, loving others will make it much easier to experience how right it feels to love yourself.

• You may also want to practise

—Meditating on love (see pp 219, 221).

—Meditating on the self of the other (see p 159).

—Expressing your love aloud without tying it to any particular action or outcome. Borrowing the behaviour you need (see p 62) may help overcome any initial awkwardness.

Thich Nhat Hanh's *Peace Is Every Step* will also support you as you tune into the radiant pleasure of giving and receiving love.

Putting yourself in the place of others

'If people generally felt what the victim feels while the lynching mob yells at the door, if they could exchange places with the haggard inmates of Belsen or Dachau, if they could enter into the dreary misery of the Siberian labour camps, then what exactly would happen, I don't know; but I do know that, somehow and soon, an order that supported these things would be blown into a million fragments.'

Brand Blanchard in *Daily Readings from Quaker Spirituality*

Reading this passage creates an opportunity to consider how your increase in self-knowledge and self-love can be mirrored by your love for others, and knowledge of others: in this case, not special 'others' in your personal life, but those who suffer hardship and persecution, starvation and death, for no greater reason than they—and not you—are in the wrong place at the wrong time.

• Envisage one of the many life-denying crises that plague our planet.

Imagine yourself in that situation. Imagine your child, your mother or a loved friend in that situation with you (dying of starvation, denied clean water, sheltering from mortar fire).

Ask your inner world to give you the strength to leave behind the safety of distance and choice just for a moment, and to be with those suffering people in their distress and torment.

• No matter how slight that experience was, allow it to harden your resolve to help in some practical way around your chosen issue: by further informing yourself and others; by giving money to an aid organisation; by taking up the issue with those in power; by showing that you care.

You may also want to send love, meditate on peace, pray for justice.

Parent-role and lover-role

It is virtually impossible to function successfully in the roles of parent and lover to the same person. This is as true for lesbian and gay male couples as it is for heterosexuals. Two people who are lovers—and who want to stay being lovers—inevitably benefit from learning to recognise when they are turning to their partner and asking that person (perhaps unconsciously) to make up for old pains, omissions and transgressions from the past.

• Take time to review whether

You are asking your partner to be your parent, your business manager, your child, your therapist—as well as your lover.

This is appropriate and comfortable *for you both*.

You can hear your partner's requests that you move closer—or back off—without anxious self-defence (see p 108).

As you muse on those questions, recall specific encounters, arguments and injured feelings. Recalling your own or your partner's accusations of insufficiency will help! ('You never try to . . .', 'Whenever I want to . . .')

Write down all your thoughts, feelings, hesitancies, confusions, insights. This may well take you way beyond an initial session.

• Later, bring your awareness to the ways in which you can take the load from your partner. Here are some ways to do that:

—Develop the strongest possible trust in your own self.

— Unravel your own emotional history.

— Know what issues from the past affect the present.

— Limit your expectations of what another person should provide.

— Take some pressing emotional needs outside the relationship: to other friends; to like-minded people who share crucial experiences (as in support groups); to a therapist or counsellor; to your own Wise Being.

• Anchor your insights with two practical resolutions which reflect

—How you can take more care of yourself.

—How you can get more care/stimulation/nourishment from people outside your sexual relationship.

Take lots of time to become aware of what you didn't get in childhood and what you resent most from your childhood. Use that awareness to be especially sensitive about *not asking* your lover for extra bonuses in those special areas, or expecting them to be provided.

Use your creativity to expand the circle where the help you want and need can be found. It is fine to talk to your lover about your insights, and to hear hers or his also. Allow time for this sharing, and for respecting any conflicting feelings that may arise.

Intimacy and independence

Does your intimacy with other people cost them the chance of having an independent life? What does having an independent life mean to you?

• Make yourself comfortable. Close your eyes and check where your body needs some attention. Slow your breath and spend a few moments breathing in and out keeping your awareness on the breath: in, out; in, out.

When you feel relatively calm, tell yourself you are going to explore two challenging questions and that you will do so with an open mind, welcoming any information you find.

• Write out the two questions above, in the first person. Write each on top of a large sheet of paper as a constant reference throughout the meditation. Rephrase them if you wish.

Does my way of being intimate cost others the chance of an independent life?

What do I think having an independent life means?

• As you explore those two questions, jot down your reactions to them then close your eyes again, letting the questions stay with you until more associations occur to you and you write again. Don't censor what you write. The oddest associations may be useful. Include emotional information as well as any information you are getting from your body: 'Men get independence more easily than women—my stomach tightens.' 'Women seem to be able to give so much support to each other and my throat is tight and it's hard to swallow. I want to get up and stop this.'

• Spend at least fifteen minutes thinking, writing; withdrawing, writing. It helps to recall specific situations and your current reactions.

Allow a further fifteen minutes to drift in a state of reverie. More information may arise. Write that down.

• At the end of the session you may be ready to make a modest resolution to reflect your respect for the independent life of others. Note that resolution. Keep it focused on a change that you will make yourself. *It is not your concern to change others.*

Shift 'I will tell Patricia she should have more time alone,' to 'It's my guilt-tripping that makes it hard for Patricia to enjoy time alone. I can stop that and talk to her about why I've been doing it.'

Shift 'I will let Michael stay after work for a drink,' to 'I will step up my own social contacts. Then I'll resent it less when Michael wants a drink.'

• Should no practical resolution present itself, simply note your readiness for change in your journal. Something will certainly occur to you, once the seed is planted. Monitor your resolve, or your intention.

Intruding on others

There is a hair-thin line between intimacy, emotional proximity and intrusion.

Whether someone feels easily intruded upon largely depends on how she or he experiences those invisible boundaries between self and other.

Whether someone is unselfconsciously intrusive largely depends on their capacity to contain or even recognise their own neediness, and thus be sensitive to others' emotional 'space' and rights to that space.

• Take this idea of 'emotional space' into your mind. Sit with it for a while. See if an image arises which expresses how you feel about it. Draw that image quickly, without censoring or analysing it. Ask it what it is ready to tell you (see p 31).

If you were sexually or emotionally abused, then this may be an extremely painful topic to recall. Take it slowly.

• Write the word SPACE on a large sheet of paper, and then jot down your associations with it. The following questions might help. As you write and think, think and write, pay attention to what is happening in your body: how you are breathing; when you feel choked up, angry or sad; tense or relaxed. Include those observations in what you write and draw.

Do you have space in which to feel your own feelings, think your own thoughts, dream your own dreams, experience your inner rhythms?

Do you have space to be creative or spontaneous in your own way without comment or criticism from others? (Such space is essential for children and adolescents, as well as for adults.)

Does something need to change before you can ask for or take the space you need?

• Do you have too much space—and with that a painful sense of isolation?

What could lessen that feeling of isolation a little? Ask your inner world for an image which may come at once, or not for a few hours or days.

• Explore what happens *in your inner world of feelings* when people come too close, or feel too far away.

Write or draw your associations, thoughts or feelings, perhaps focusing on one or two memories at a time. Move slowly. This is a big issue for many people.

• Perhaps you fill up space when you are with others: vocally, emotionally, physically, intellectually.

How would it be to step back a little? (Fantasise doing that and note down your thoughts and feelings. Formulate a simple strategy—maybe nothing more dramatic than slowing your breathing and checking out what is happening in the present.)

• Do you feel powerless when others fill emotional and physical space in those ways?

How would it be to assert yourself a little more? (Again, see yourself in an imagined situation, checking out what you need—see p 85.)

• Should you want to explore more deeply, take a couple of sessions to recall, draw and write about how this vital and usually unspoken issue of emotional space was experienced in your family of origin.

Who was allowed physical space? Privacy? A chance to speak? Who established the rules about body boundaries? About how time was used? About approved and disapproved activities, attitudes, beliefs? About food? About cleanliness?

Write about the issues in the first person. They may become clearer if you write from the perspective of when you were especially sensitive to infringements. This may well be when you entered adolescence. ('Grandad has no idea how much I hate it when he . . .') Write for at least fifteen minutes, with a further fifteen minutes for reflection.

• *Acknowledge how the situation is different for you now.*

Review what choices you have now that you did not have as a child. Write down any discoveries you make, no matter how apparently trivial.

('I don't have to agree with my mother. I can get up when I want. I can sit with my legs apart. I can get excited about issues I care about. I can sleep in a room by myself. I refuse to be whined at.')

Translate at least one of those discoveries into a resolution. Support your resolution with active meditations.

'I don't always have to listen to other people when I am tired.' (See p 119.)

'I can choose to waste time dreaming.' (See p 143.)

'My life does not belong to other people.' (See p 70.)

'I will try to let others come closer.' (See p 180.)

'Make me happy!'

Do you resent your partner, your child or your parents *when they fail to make you happy*? Or maybe it is your employer who is failing you, or the political system, or God? Check out who or what you most commonly blame or rail against and then write to that person or entity.

• Use Free Writing (see p 32) to explore this crazy and extremely common demand. Your guiding sentence could be, 'You should make me happy because . . .' Write for at least fifteen minutes. As you write, check out what is happening in your body. Include those observations in your writing too.

'You should make me happy because I've a pain in my back and my eyes hurt.'

'You should make me happy because I am sick of that din next door on the building site . . .'

• When you feel 'written out' and reasonably humbled by the power you are giving away, take back that power!

Bring to your conscious awareness the knowledge that other people can affect your happiness, *but are not responsible for it*.

You are mistress or master of your own happiness.

Float with that thought for at least another fifteen minutes. Breathe it in; breathe it out. Say it softly, loudly; sing it, whisper it.

• If you now feel willing to be responsible for your own happiness, anchor that thought by writing it down.

Maybe you will need a reminder: an image, a drawing, lines from a poem or the words 'My happiness' written onto card. Put your reminder where you will see it on waking.

In your next self-therapy session, pick up this crucial issue again.

• Bring to your conscious awareness the realisation that *you can affect others' happiness*, even while you are not responsible for it. Acting with this awareness reflects your capacity for self-responsibility.

Float with that thought for at least fifteen minutes. Feel it flow through your body as well as swirling it around in your mind. Review some recent experiences. How do they seem now?

• Is there any small change you want to make in your attitude or behaviour with others? Write that down to anchor it and bring it into immediate effect in your daily life.

Keep it to yourself

There is a tremendous impulse within many relationships to have everything out in the open: opinions, experiences, attitudes and moods. There is certainly a place for being open, for sharing feelings, for looking together at what is happening and working on strategies when conflicts are causing one or more people pain. But there is also a place for holding back that impulse to engage someone else in what may be an internal struggle, or conflict within yourself.

Daryl Sharp affirms this point of view in his book, *The Survival Papers*, a most interesting, readable account of a Jungian analysis that is nevertheless itself unselfconsciously sexist. However, there are some gems in the book and the following lines are well worth considering—at least some of the time.

'You work on a relationship by shutting your mouth when you are ready to explode. By not afflicting your affect [an open display of your feelings, some of which may arise from past situations] on the other person. By quietly leaving the battlefield and tearing your hair out. By asking yourself—and not your partner—what complex in you was activated, and to what end. The proper question is not, "Why is he or she doing that to me?" or "Who do they think they are?" but rather, "Why am I acting in this way?—Who do *I* think they are?" And more: "What does this say about my psychology? What can I do about it?"'

• Take time in your self-therapy session to think anew about the pattern of conflict between yourself and someone close to you (your lover, parent, child).

• Notice as you review that pattern when it might follow feelings of disturbance or uncertainty within you.

Is it possible that you avoid such uncertainty by concentrating on the other person and the wrongs they are doing to you?

Now recall an actual fight or argument. How much energy on your side goes into letting the other person know how they have failed you, how they are responsible for your pain and unhappiness, how they are keeping you from the life you could be living, if only . . .

Notice how intensely you feel old pain as well as new pain at this moment. You may also feel ashamed, resentful, confused, desperate: all of which you may long for the other person to notice and acknowledge, even while you are telling them how much you hate or despise or mistrust them.

• Spend time reviewing what specific painful feelings emerge for you in this kind of encounter.

Now write about them, or draw a symbol for them that emerges from within as you experience again the memories of that kind of encounter.

John drew a cave which was damp and empty and completely inhospitable. Looking at it he was able to say, 'It's when I feel I am alone in that cave and have no way of getting out of it that I get most angry with my lover. But I can't say, "I feel lonely. I am in a cave." Instead I just pick on him so that he then tells me what a whingeing and demanding person I am which aptly reflects that lonely, needy soul sitting in the darkness of the cave but it is the very last thing I want to hear. It makes me desperate.'

• Now see yourself again at the brink of a typical painful encounter.

Reason is about to be lost; good sense is flying out of the window. Your pulse is racing. Nothing matters but your urge to be proved right. Yet despite all those reasons to stay and shoot it out, *this time you withdraw.*

See yourself getting right away from the temptation to externalise your inner pain: into your bedroom if you can lock the door, into the bathroom, or, if you can leave the house safely, to a park or cafe. There you can sit and ask yourself the questions suggested above by Daryl Sharp.

Doing so, you bring the focus back onto yourself in a truly self-responsible way—while also saving yourself from a heavy dose of retaliatory anger. It may also help to ask the following questions. Write out your answers, taking all the time you need.

Why am I angry right now?

What is behind my anger?

What conflict in me am I not recognising?

What do I need that I am not getting?

How can I ask for what I need, rather than hoping my needs will be recognised and met through a painful encounter?

Is this a need I can take care of myself, or in some other way?

• Next time a quarrel is brewing, refuse it, trying this strategy instead. The strong feelings you want to express will not be denied, but you will have understood them better and will be able to express them more appropriately at a time when there are fewer dark clouds overhead.

Even when you are convinced that what is going on is a relationship issue rather than a problem within yourself, fighting it out is rarely going to get you what you want. These lines might clarify this further. They are also from Daryl Sharp.

'On the whole, you work on a relationship by keeping your mood to yourself and examining it. You neither bottle up the emotion nor allow it to poison the relationship. The merit in this approach is that it throws us back entirely on our experience of ourselves. It is foolish to imagine we can change the person who seems to be the cause of our heartache. But with the proper container we can change ourselves and our reactions.'

Clearing hurt and anger

Do you feel forced to behave dishonestly with someone who has hurt or angered you? Must you see that person regularly or within a context where civility is demanded?

It is possible to make those encounters clearer and more comfortable through your efforts alone, without involving the other person.

• Deepen your understanding about your feelings by drawing an image for the way *you feel about the person*. The image might be unpleasant. (This is only the first stage.) If you want to add words, do so.

• On a fresh sheet of paper, draw two images, one of which stands for yourself in this relationship, and one for the other person.

Look at those two images, how they sit on the page in relation to each other (close or far apart? one big, one small?); at the colours you have chosen for each; at what each points up about the other one.

• Ask each image if it can help the other one to clear the air or find a way forward (see p 31). Take time to talk and to listen. When the two images have told each other all they can, ask each one to tell *you* how your situation could ease right now, today, in the present.

• You may want to write in the first person, *as each image*: 'When I look at you I think of . . .'

• Now see yourself in a fresh encounter with this person. You have new information, at least about the dynamic between you. How does that new information alter or shift what happens?

Note any thoughts you have, or any strategy that will benefit you without adversely affecting the other person involved.

Until you feel clearer in the relationship, continue to draw such images, watching how and when they change, what different energy is evoked as your feelings rise closer to the surface.

• Later, you may want to turn from drawing to writing.

Address the person directly, as though writing a letter, but using a repeated guiding sentence which might be:

'I will never forgive you for . . .'

'When I see you I feel flooded with memories of the time when . . .'

It may take several self-therapy sessions to get beyond that sentence. Be patient. Something else will emerge, or you will find that the energy it takes to think fierce, negative thoughts about that person is not with you any longer.

Whatever you write, and however justified your hurt feels, DO NOT MAIL THIS COMMUNICATION.

If you are tempted to send it, destroy it instead. This will leave you empty of negative energy, and at greater peace with yourself (see p 113).

Who or what do you talk about?

• Using any recent day in your life as an example, increase your awareness about *the content* of what you say. Explore the following questions as a way to increase self-knowledge. Give each one a couple of minutes at least.

Are you most engaged or eloquent when talking about yourself?

Do you avoid ever talking about yourself?

Are your partner and children the people you talk about most—or exclusively?

Do you talk about others in a way that attempts to make you look good?

Do you talk most about people and relationships?

Are you ever comfortable talking about people and relationships?

Do you have pet topics to which you consistently return (work, money, sport, politics)?

Are there subject areas you find intolerable and deflect or disparage in others?

Is the energy of your talking largely positive or negative?

• When you have spent time writing down your thoughts and feelings that arise in answer to these questions, take time to discover if your vital self/other balance is in need of attention.

Do you need to broaden your awareness beyond yourself and your immediate concerns?

Do you need the courage to focus your awareness back onto yourself and your immediate concerns?

• Make a small resolution to anchor what you have discovered. Promise yourself to monitor that resolution.

Are you aware that it is often easier for two people to experience their intimacy with each other by talking about a third person (perhaps one of their own children), rather than what is going on between the two of them? Sometimes it feels necessary for them to ally themselves together *against* a third person (or an outside force of some kind) in order to feel united.

It is worth exploring whether in addition to talking about other people, and thus forging your alliance, it is possible also to
—Express what you are thinking and feeling *about each other*.
—Risk saying what you want or need *from each other*.

The intimate listening exercises will help (see pp 196, 197).

Trade-offs (1)

An intimate relationship can be blighted because one party is especially annoyed by *this* behaviour, while the other party is distressed by *that*. This can be true between lovers, between family members (parent/child) and between close friends.

When there is goodwill and honesty between people it is possible to identify those behaviours and to agree to *give up* a behaviour that troubles the other person in exchange for their giving up a behaviour that troubles you.

For example, I can't stand your sulking, you can't stand the way I belittle other people. We agree that you won't sulk, I won't belittle.

• Take time—laced with lots of goodwill!—to identify what each of you most wants the other one to give up. (Now is not the time to take offence. Improvements are in sight.)

Agree what your trade-off will be, and how and when you will review it.

Support each other in this trade-off. Don't give up in the face of the odd bit of backsliding, but do have it as part of your separate and shared consciousness that *it is of value to you both* to give up a behaviour that is diminishing the quality of an important relationship.

It may be rewarding to do this exercise concurrently with Lucy Goodison's meditation (see p 161).

Trade-offs (2)

Are you and your partner predominantly thinking or feeling people?

When stressed, the thinking person is likely to become more rigidly 'rational' (and out of touch), while the feeling person is likely to experience a flood of feeling and possibly confusion and powerlessness.

If this kind of split between feeling and thinking reflects your relationship pattern under stress, you can decrease such stress by agreeing *in advance* to exchange your key words next time you find yourselves on the brink of war.

• The thinking person will agree to start all her sentences with 'I feel . . .' and be true to that statement by stretching herself to know what she feels (and that she can feel).

• The feeling person will agree to start all her sentences with: 'I think . . .' and will be true to that statement by stretching herself to find out what she thinks (and that she can think).

This will develop in each of you a stronger sense of self, and a more alive sense of the other, by

—Each stretching her capacities to think *and* feel.

—Each bringing her awareness to whether and how she needs to further develop her thinking or feeling function.

—Each honouring and supporting her partner to think, or feel, a little more flexibly.

• You can rehearse the strategy by deciding on a topic that is not painful but arouses reasonably strong feelings in each of you. As you discuss it, monitor your own progress in sticking to 'I think' or 'I feel' as agreed. Afterwards discuss where you began to lose track or feel overcome by old patterns.

• You may want to end each session on this most useful topic by withdrawing to explore Living with the Rose (see p 46). Share what you discover minimally, not analysing the other person's experience, but simply accepting it with love and interest.

Fears in the present; losses in the past

Unexpectedly, it is often when we are in an intimate relationship that repressed feelings of loss, betrayal, the fear of being abandoned or overwhelmed come to the surface. They may push us into defensive behaviours which we unconsciously believe will save us from those self-threatening feelings overwhelming us. You, for example, may be withdrawn and prickly with the person you love most; critical, angry, bitchy or abusive—in an attempt to protect your vulnerable core.

Those fears in the present almost always have a history that traces back to when you were a small child, or perhaps an infant, without the capacity you now have to take a broader view of your life, to respond flexibly, to know that you can—when you need to—take good care of yourself.

Here is a long active meditation which will allow you to acknowledge those fears and bring them out into the open where they are much less likely to drive you into self-defeating behaviours. Take your time. It is likely to extend over a number of sessions and recalling a fragment of information at a time may be quite enough.

- Use the quiet space of your self-therapy to identify your fears.

  Perhaps you have none?

  Yet you always end a relationship before someone else can?

  Or you are careful, even guarded about confiding in others?

  Or you know it is foolish to trust others?

  Or you don't bring sex and love into the same relationship?

  Or you prioritise work, seeing it as safer than the messy world of personal relationships?

  Or you act negatively or in self-defeating ways with the people who matter most?

- Consider those common fears again: loss, betrayal, the fear of being abandoned, the fear of being overwhelmed.

  Over several sessions you can explore all those fears. You may want to begin with loss.

  Quickly draw an image for the way you feel about loss.

  Should you feel stuck, ask your Wise Being (see p 23) for an image to help you understand what loss means to you now, in the present. Later you may want to ask for an image to help you understand what loss meant to you in the past.

- When the drawing is finished, note your feelings as you drew: cold, excited, distanced, nervous, unwilling to draw.

• Look again at the image you have drawn. Ask it what you need to understand; why this image has come to you and not another. Write down whatever thoughts and associations arise in your mind.

If you have two images, one for the present experience and one for the past, allow those images to speak to each other.

• Now you can write in your journal *as loss* (see p 31), using the first person.

Here is what Hilary wrote. 'I look like this big white ball. I look quite snowy and soft but actually as I roll downhill I get larger and larger. I need to be kept out of sight, but I'm always ready to roll. I am the snowball effect. Let me get going and there'll be no stopping me. For a snowball I have an incredible head of steam. I am laughing. But I am not funny, I'm cold and want to be warmer.'

• In a following session, use Free Writing (see p 32) to intensify your exploration. Your guiding sentence could be 'The way I now feel about loss . . .' or 'I still avoid thinking about loss because . . .' Persist for at least fifteen minutes and allow another fifteen minutes for musing and possible further writing.

In separate sessions, move through other emotions: betrayal, fear of being abandoned, fear of being overwhelmed—or any other intense anxieties you want to understand more deeply.

Take time to explore your feelings in the past as well as in the present. If you feel sad, or empty of feeling and energy as you do this meditation, then promise yourself to return to it, but *slowly and with love*, while also freely Borrowing the behaviour you need (see p 62) and Meditating on the quality you most desire (see p 145).

Finding your centre

'By birthright, each of us is the centre of our own world. But how often do we lose that sense and believe that the centre is in Paris, the Moscow of the Three Sisters, the Oxford of Jude the Obscure; or the Coral Islands of the

Pacific, or the source of the Ganges, or the party to which
we were not invited. That sense of here-and-now eludes
us, and we pursue it, never happy until we overtake it, if
we ever do. For the world is full of exiles — perhaps nearly
all of us are exiles for nearly all of our lives.'

Kathleen Raine, *Farewell Happy Fields*

Breathe in; breathe out.
This is it. This is now. This is all.
Breathe in; breathe out.
This is all.

Recycling your strengths

Your attitude towards yourself directs others (perhaps unconsciously)
to how they should experience you. Are there some areas of your
life where you are not experienced as you would like to be?

You can use Free Writing (see p 32) and Free Drawing (see p 30)
to create a mirror. See yourself in that mirror, freshly revealed in a
variety of situations. You can then recycle strengths to where they
are needed.

• Start with Free Writing. Your guiding sentence could be 'Others
see me as . . .' or 'When I am with other people I am . . .' Recall a
variety of situations when you interact with others: at home, work,
socially.

• Now allow images to arise that describe how others see you.
This may differ from how you experience yourself on the inside.
Then draw two images, side by side. Again, break down relationships into specific kinds: with women, men, children, at work, at
the club, casual, family, neighbourhood, and so on.

Gail said, 'Thinking about how others see me at school functions I drew a big mouth carefully outlined in bright red lipstick.
It looked rather awesome and potentially overwhelming. Thinking
about how I feel at those functions, I drew plaits that were tightly
braided and tied with neat, thin ribbons. That was a very subdued
image and I wonder if I'm overcompensating.'

• Having written and drawn all you can, spread your pages around you. Perhaps some themes—and strengths—are immediately clear, or you may need to formulate a question or two and let those simmer in your mind until a later session: How do I appear? What signals am I giving out? How do I want to change that?

• When there is one area or more in your life where you want change, locate another area where you feel more content and *borrow a strength from that area.*

Formulate your insight, making it practical and specific. Write your resolve in your journal.

'I intend to be as careful in my listening at home as I am with my customers.'

'I can make allowances for my women friends in the same way I make allowances for male friends.'

'I am assertive with my children but not my parents and will change that.'

• Take time regularly to continue recycling your emotional strengths!

Picking up emotional litter

Be conscious that no matter how individually powerless you may feel at any moment, your thoughts, behaviour and feelings affect other people. You cannot think, act, react, feel or respond without affecting your environment.

• Take a few moments each day to ask yourself three simple but significant questions.

What emotional litter am I leaving behind?

Am I looking around with awareness and 'picking up' as I go?

Is there any small change I should instantly make?

Respecting other people's dramas

You call a friend. She is abrupt and anxious to get off the phone.

Do you wonder what is going on with her?

Do you assume you have done something wrong?

Do you curse her for her lack of consideration for your feelings?

Do you shrug and accept it?

This active meditation can offer useful insights into your self/other dynamics, especially when you feel upset by a personal exchange that feels uncomfortable or 'not right', or when you don't have a clear sense of what's going on between yourself and another person.

• Start by recalling two or three recent situations when someone else was distressed, angry, abrupt or dismissive and you felt confused or locked out.

Write down your reactions, and what assumptions you made.

Did you worry that it must be your fault? Did you blame the other person for their rudeness? Did you feel hurt, offended, guilty, angry? Did you want to protect yourself—or the other person?

Were your feelings typical (for you) of that kind of encounter?

• Run one of those situations through your mind again, this time exploring how it might feel for you to stay far enough back from the situation to react spontaneously, yet close enough to be available if that is needed.

Now see yourself acknowledging that you are witnessing an upset, but that upset 'belongs' to someone else, and not to you.

Can you do that? Does it feel good (for you, and for the other person)?

Perhaps what I'm suggesting here is difficult even to imagine. Perhaps you are uncomfortably aware that your reaction was judgemental or self-protective—and that it will be next time also.

Use that insight as a learning opportunity.

If you are unable to act with genuine concern for others—and detachment when that is called for—it is not because you are a bad person. It is probably because you feel envious or unlovable, depressed or powerless. That is not a comfortable way to feel but your self-therapy is allowing you to build sufficient self-love and respect to have some spare for others.

Use the strength and wisdom of your Wise Being (see p 23).

Use the Meditations on love (see pp 219, 221). Allow them to work for you.

• If you feel ready, you can explore what happens for you when you offer support and it is rejected. Again, recall a couple of specific situations that are recent, or powerful enough to have stayed in your memory. As you run those situations through in your mind, lovingly observe whether you can

—Step aside from feeling that you have been personally rejected ('My support isn't good enough.').

—Avoid the temptation to blame ('That silly bitch has never known what's good for her.').

—Check if you have indeed caused distress ('I can hear you're upset and I wonder if there's anything I've done that we should talk about.').

If you have no reason to believe that the distress or remoteness is caused by you, visualise removing yourself from the centre of the drama!

Offer support when that seems appropriate ('I can hear you're upset. Is there anything you'd like to talk about?'), but resist the temptation to take offence if the person is not ready, or prefers support from someone else.

Taking offence re-positions you *in your own mind* at the centre of the drama. That is rarely the best vantage point.

Bring your awareness back to the central issue: this is someone else's drama, not your own.

Too many demands

Being in good contact with yourself, allows you to be in good contact with others. And being in good contact with others, being fed internally by others, allows you to be alone without feeling lonely.

You may feel angry, worn down or depleted, demented and non-sexual, lacking in flexibility and generosity . . . for no worse reason than because your life is overcrowded. (I am horribly familiar with this problem, and continue to find it extremely difficult to modify. But it is worth persisting; I am sure of that.)

Check out what demands you are meeting: your own and other people's.

• Write each demand on a separate card.

• Spread the cards around you in a big circle.

• Give each card a mark out of ten. Ten for absolute essentials (food, sleep, time with the children, earning money) down to nought for things that are somewhat crazy (spending time with people you don't like, doing extra work to impress other people).

• When you have a clearer sense of your priorities, decide to cancel a few obligations.

On those cards write, large and in a bright colour, I WILL NO LONGER . . . iron my adult son's shirts; I WILL NO LONGER . . . go to the office on Sunday mornings; I WILL NO LONGER . . . always fill in when others have emergencies.

• Where you see there are demands in your life that you can and do want to meet, or genuinely must meet, accept those.

Write on those cards: I AM WILLING TO . . . cook dinner six nights a week; I AM WILLING TO . . . take my children to Saturday sports; I AM WILLING TO . . . put in extra time at work for the next five years.

• Review the situation regularly. Watch whether your pile of cards is going up or down. Watch whether you are beginning to feel *unwilling* around some of your activities.

Your significant others are separate people

For when we love, we have no
other choice
but to let each other go.

Rainer Maria Rilke, 'Requiem for a Friend'

Caring intensely about someone does not mean crashing through self/other boundaries. Yet many of us feel as sensitive about criticisms made of our significant others (spouses, children, parents) as we do about criticism of ourselves. Or we feel painfully dependent on someone else doing well so we can feel proud or even happy.

There is no psychological harm done by rejoicing in appreciation of your loved ones, or feeling your hackles rise when they are criticised, but it is vital for their good health, and your own, that you can experience yourself and your loved ones as people whose needs, actions and feelings deeply affect each other, but may not always be congruent.

• Settle yourself, while knowing you may be tackling an uncomfortable topic. Tell yourself you are ready to do that at an appropriate pace. The goal is to be no less loving, just more flexible. Check you are relaxed, taking your breath deep into your body before letting it go again.

• Recall a time when you felt crushed because someone you love was misjudged, overlooked or criticised. See that situation like a film on a screen you can watch from a safe distance. Slow it down to monitor your reactions. As you watch, review these questions and jot down any thoughts or feelings that arise.

Did you feel an injury had been done to your own self?

What was your dominant emotion? Your dominant thought?

What was happening in your body at that time?

Were you able to be supportive of your loved one?

Did you feel you had to be protective of your loved one?

Did you give more weight to the criticism than to your own knowledge?

Were you angry about being 'shown up' or embarrassed?

How would your reactions have been different if the person criticised was less closely involved with you, and you with him or her?

• Look back to the screen again. Is there anything else you have missed?

Write down all your thoughts and feelings, no matter how contradictory or fragmented. Take at least fifteen minutes to write and fifteen minutes to reflect about this and similar situations. More thoughts might arise as you ponder.

• Is there one practical resolution you feel ready to make to express your awareness *that each person is entitled to their own experiences, mistakes, crises and conflicts so she or he has their chance to learn and grow?*

Write that resolution down as one simple sentence in your journal. Take time to monitor it and support yourself through what may be a difficult shift in attitude.

The rewards of negative emotions

Some people carry a righteous load of anger, hostility, resentment or any other bleak emotion for many years *and all their intimate or quasi-intimate relationships are deeply affected by it.*

The first wife who can never forgive the second wife for 'going off with' her husband; the parents of a child who 'marries out' of their particular race or set of beliefs; the unemployed worker whose life has been ruined by his redundancy; the adult child whose life is tainted by parental emotional incompetence or abuse; all these people are entitled to whatever their particular expression of frustration may be, but when that emotion persists and colours their lives, it is worth exploring what the benefits are of holding on.

Take time to explore these questions—with an open mind and heart. You may want to record this meditation, allowing plenty of time for musing and writing.

• Think about a situation where you are holding on to a negative emotion or attitude. Is it

—Keeping you connected to the person or situation you are unhappy about?

—More acceptable than pain or loss or resignation?

—Allowing you to feel important (as you 'maintain the rage')?

—Justifying your unpleasant, demanding or self-pitying behaviour?

—Giving meaning or purpose to your life?

Jot down any thoughts or feelings that occur to you, however unexpected or uncomfortable these are.

• When you have some understanding of what holding on is doing for you, ask yourself if you are willing to get those same benefits in some other, less harmful way.

If the answer is yes, visualise your 'holding on' energy. A visual image will tell you how much energy this is: a bucketful, a tonne, a lorryload, a skyscraper's worth?

• As you look at your bucket or ten-tonne truck, you will see that attached to it is a label that describes *the emotion you are surrendering*. See yourself tearing off the label. (You will find a ladder nearby in your imagination, if you need it.)

• Now see yourself putting up another label. When you look closely, this label describes a positive emotion (hope, patience, tenacity, flexibility, forgiveness, compassion) that will serve you and those closest to you.

When you have identified what's on that label, *and have appreciated how much of that emotion is available to you*, ask yourself what change in attitude this new feeling might allow.

• Frame a simple, practical resolve.

'With a bathful of tenacity I can face the rounds of jobsearching again.'

'An oil tanker's worth of laughter will ease the limitations of my relationship with Henry.'

• If you cannot yet identify a positive activity, plant the seed by writing a sentence similiar to this one: 'With so much (hope, trust, humour) available to me, my mind is open to new inspiration.'

'*I am not my negative emotions*'

I have anger. *I am not my anger*.
  I feel angry. *I am not my anger*.
  I feel self-hating. *I am not my self-hatred*.
  I am full of hate. *I am not my hatred*.

I am envious. *I am not my envy.*

I am bursting with jealousy. *I am not my jealousy.*

I feel depressed. *I am not my depression.*

These lines allow you to acknowledge distressing feelings—and also disidentify from them.

• Adapt them freely, then take the time to write them out or speak them aloud. You are reminding yourself that your negative emotions are something *you express*, not who you are. Keeping a sense of separateness between yourself and those painful emotions does reduce their power. Gradually you can begin to express them with choice. As you grow in self-understanding and love, their tentacles will weaken.

Observing your anger

Here is another excellent way to harness your awareness as your ally and change a behaviour which is impeding you. My example is observing and diminishing anger as anger fuels—even justifies—so much violence; but you can adapt it to any unrewarding behaviour.

• Visualise yourself angry. See yourself on a big screen you are watching from a safe distance. Notice that your attention is focused obsessively on the current trigger for your anger. This remains true *even when your anger is exacerbated by rage from the past.*

• Look at yourself on the big screen again. Ask yourself what the trigger might have recalled for you. Here is what Janice said.

'I heard a certain tone in Will's voice which reminded me—although it was unconscious at the time—of the contemptuous way I was spoken to as a child. That tone triggered my anger and *I hated Will.*'

Janice's rage seemed perfectly justified in the present, but it belonged—in considerable measure—to the past. When Will protested, he did not calm the situation; he further fuelled Janice's anger.

• You—like Janice—can avoid that obsessive attention, and the rapid escalation that accompanies it, by choosing to turn your attention *away from* the trigger (the person, the noise, the mess in your child's bedroom, the empty gin bottle, the syringe) and *instead observing your anger*.

• Rehearse this in your self-therapy session, seeing yourself again up on the big screen, but this time turning away and *observing your anger*.

Don't criticise it, or yourself. Just watch it. Be aware: 'I am very, very angry.'

• Slow your breathing. Watch the anger. Just watch it.

• If you need to, see yourself withdrawing *physically* from the trigger.

Go walking, go to your room, lock yourself in the bathroom. You are not denying your anger by withdrawing. You are refusing to fuel it. It is always possible to return to the situation when you are less angry and share your feelings about what caused you distress.

• Visualise that you will be left with a strong feeling of empowerment, and much less emotional mess to clean up.

Next time you are angry, put into practice what you have rehearsed. If it doesn't work for you immediately, don't lose heart. Rehearse the steps again, notice where you lost your way, and continue to keep anger where it belongs: as one of many emotions you are entitled to feel but one that does not rule you.

'I am entitled to my anger because . . .'

Why do you get angry (or depressed, sulky, vengeful, jealous, envious)? What is your anger doing for you? Is there any function anger has you are not ready to give up? Could you continue to feel entitled to the emotion, but less burdened by expressing it? The following meditation allows you to explore those questions. And as habits of thought and reaction can be tough to throw off, know you can return to it as often as you want.

If you are someone who cannot feel or express anger—and this is true for many women who have been told that anger is not 'nice'—speak as though anger were part of your emotional entitlement. You may be surprised by how your anger emerges in other guises.

When possible, do this active meditation with another person. That person should keep eye contact with you when you want that, and display an attitude of acceptance without judgement. The listener should not comment on what you are saying, nor question you about it, nor advise you—*either during or after the meditation*.

Perhaps you do not have someone you can trust to listen in that way? There are two equally useful ways to make this exploration.

1 You can 'tell' your Wise Being (see p 23). If she/he 'comments', then listen! This is quite different from someone speaking to you about your experience—with the voice of their experience.

2 You can write down what you might otherwise say, or speak it into a tape recorder, imagining you are preparing it for an ideal listener.

Set aside at least fifteen minutes for speaking (or writing) even if some of that time you are silent (or not writing). You will need at least the same amount of time to write in your journal afterwards.

• Take time to slow your breathing. Tell yourself you are going to make some valuable discoveries at the pace that will serve you best.

Either write or speak, saying, 'I am entitled to my anger because . . .' Avoid lengthy sidetracks. Whenever you need to, return to your guiding phrase, 'I am entitled to my anger because . . .'

• After speaking, write down what you observed and felt during the meditation and *how you feel now that it is over*.

What was the most useful insight you gained? Write that out.

• Is there any shift in feeling or attitude you want to bring into your daily life? Can you formulate that as a practical resolve, and note it in your journal?

Don't be discouraged if you make no discoveries beyond the most obvious. Louise persisted, despite almost overwhelming feelings of resistance (experienced as irritation that itself verged on anger). Eventually she blurted out, 'I am entitled to my anger because it makes me as powerful as my father.'

Having discovered that, she was slowly able to recall other ways her father was powerful with which she could more fruitfully identify.

Not rage, but . . .

Sometimes anger is a legitimate response. But when you are chronically angry, when your angry feelings seem out of proportion to the trigger that provoked your anger, or when angry feelings linger to pollute your contacts with others, then it's worth exploring what lies behind your anger, remembering that it is often more acceptable to your conscious mind to feel anger than grief or loss, inadequacy or helplessness.

• Recall a recent or memorable situation when you felt angry.

Play a film of what happened on a big screen in your mind. You can watch with relative detachment. Use slow motion and stop on pause whenever you see your anger is stepping up.

What is happening outside yourself? How are you feeling inside? Jot down your observations before allowing the film to roll again.

• Now experiment with deeper feelings and triggers.

Bring to your awareness the emotions *you don't usually express* and the feelings *you ought not to have*. Write those down. Do any seem to fit?

• Re-run the scene, giving yourself permission to discover what was going on at a deeper level.

You might want to ask the anger to transform into the emotion it was masking. (Your Magic Wand could help.)

• When you sense what that emotion may be, write about the scene, using the new emotion where you would have written angry.

'I came into the room and as soon as I saw the mess I felt really *ashamed* and let down. Then the kids came home with their demands and I felt even more *ashamed*. Then Jacob started to bitch about the kids not helping out and by that time I was so *ashamed* I could do nothing but scream.'

• Slowly formulate a practical resolve that next time anger arises to mask a deeper emotion, you will
—Bring your awareness to the situation.
—Try to acknowledge that deeper emotion.
—Ask for whatever help you need *for that emotion*. This help may not come from your emotional environment. Focusing on the compassionate gaze of your Wise Being (see p 23) can give you a breathing space, or simply a reminder that *this too will change*.

Hurling your anger into the ocean of life

This meditation is adapted from Starhawk's *The Spiral Dance*. It is best done beside moving water—at the ocean, a lake or a river. With a small change of wording, it could be used by people who want to feel free of negative emotions other than anger.

Choose a stone which seems to suit the weight and texture of your anger.

Visualise white light entirely encircling your body.

Hold the stone in your hands and raise it to your forehead.

Concentrate and project all your anger into the stone.

When you feel ready, hurl the stone out of the circle of white light and into the water. Say

With this stone
Anger be gone.
Water bind it,
No one find it.
Earth the power.

In your mind's eye, let the circle of light surrounding you gradually disperse.

Intimate listening

The capacity to listen to what another person is saying, to take in both their words and also the meanings which lie behind the words, is crucial to intimacy. It is a skill which is at the heart of acknowledging that what is going on in someone else's inner world *matters*.

Few people are naturally intimate listeners. Other people's statements are unconsciously experienced as cues for the listener to speak; as memory jolts to an anecdote that caps the speaker's story; as the start of a battle for attention or control. But listening is a skill which can be learned, and it can transform your understanding and experience of intimacy.

For this exercise you do need a partner, although for the variation on the next page, you can work independently.

Return to this exercise until you believe the quality of your listening fully expresses your selfhood—and your awareness of the selfhood of the person speaking. The ultimate goal would be to be able to listen this way as a matter of course. And, along with that, to be able to listen *with awareness* to yourself (no easy matter!).

Set aside at least forty minutes without interruptions.

• Choose a topic of interest to you both: what it was like growing up in your family; how you feel about your work; a recreational or philosophical interest; what's happening now in your relationships; how you are feeling about yourself; whether or how you feel your life should open out.

• Sit comfortably facing each other. Take a few calming, aware breaths.

• The first person should talk—or simply occupy the silence— for ten to fifteen minutes (agree on the time before you start).

• The second person should *do nothing but listen*. This listening should be active rather than passive, taking in what the speaker is saying, noting the speaker's changes of mood, ease in speaking, body movements, gestures and so on. The listener should also be aware of what is being conveyed by the speaker: a sense of occasion, of confusion, loss, exhilaration and so on.

The listener must not respond, interrupt or speak.

• When the agreed time is up, do not burst into a 'normal' conversation. Instead, swap roles so that the speaker becomes the listener and the listener the speaker.

• Only after both people have been speaker and listener should you share experiences. You should not comment on what has been said. Comment only on *how it felt to be a silent, attentive listener*.

• Take time to write for a few minutes in your journal about the experience of intimate listening. Promise yourself to develop this crucial skill.

Listening with awareness

Following on from Intimate listening (see above), and not leaving that practice behind, take several weeks to increase awareness of your patterns of listening.

• Notice

—What you can listen to with care and attention.

—Whether (and when) you can restrain yourself from cutting in or from drifting off.

—If your impulse is to speak (take over) rather than to listen.

—How your patterns of listening change according to the way you feel about a person and their relative 'importance' to you.

—When you feel 'entitled' to interrupt, or not.

—If you can listen to yourself with awareness.

• As you become tuned in to where your listening skills need sharpening, or making more subtle, you can rehearse what is needed during self-therapy sessions. For example, you could visualise yourself

—Listening with patience in the expectation that something of value will be shared about the speaker's experience.

—Refraining from interrupting—using awareness as your ally.

—Concentrating your attention on what is being said, rather than on what you will say next.

—Giving feedback on what has been said and conveyed, rather than taking the attention immediately back to yourself.

Practise what you have rehearsed. Observe in what situations your strategies are working, and how you feel about being a better listener. You may want to notice what you are 'hearing' for the first time (not the words only, but the feelings or intentions that lie behind them).

You will fail often. Don't be discouraged. Simply go back to the processes of visualising and persist. You may be unravelling bad habits of a lifetime, but listening well is a richly rewarding habit *that can be learned*.

'I can't listen'

Does active, caring listening seem virtually impossible for you? This does not mean that intimacy is a lost cause for you. It does indicate that giving time to someone else is—for the moment—a problem, perhaps because 'giving time' is hard when 'getting time' has been problematic.

• Recall your family's patterns of talking and of listening. Remember who listened to you in your childhood; whether listening was part of the family culture; what taboos there were on 'suitable' subject matter; whether talking (and not listening) was a way of taking control.

Recalling family meals and outings, the body language used by family members; knowing whether you sat together during leisure times or retreated to your own rooms; hearing again the tone of voice used by family members with each other; exploring how much or even whether communication was valued: this will all increase your awareness of how and why listening is difficult for you in the present.

Write down whatever you remember about those listening patterns. As you persist, unexpected memories will emerge.

Visualise yourself as a child wanting to tell an individual member of your family something important. How was that? What was positive about it—and difficult? Work your way slowly around the family, 'talking to' each person in your fantasy and reclaiming old memories.

With a clearer picture of your experiences in childhood, it may be possible for you to begin Intimate listening (see p 196).

• The following affirmation is also encouraging. Or compose one for yourself to affirm that childhood patterns need not rule your adult experience.

As an adult, I can choose to listen with care.

As an adult, I can say no to listening when that seems appropriate.

As an adult, I can afford to let someone else have time to talk.

As an adult, I appreciate that intimate listening brings me closer to others.

As an adult, I can choose to be curious.

As an adult, I can listen first, speak later.

Saying no to listening

As you increase your capacity to listen to what someone else is saying—and to what drives your own words—your relationship to others will change. *Temporarily forgetting yourself so you can listen to others brings you closer to them and strengthens your sense of self.*

This does not mean that you must become an aquiescent listener. On the contrary, as your self-knowledge grows, you may become aware of situations where you do not want to be listening.

• Visualise yourself in such a situation. Perhaps it is with someone you know is persistently malicious or critical. It may be someone you love who in times of pain or self-doubt attacks you (see p 205).

See yourself withdrawing from the situation.

Hear yourself saying, 'I am sorry, but I don't want to listen to this.'

You are entitled to choose what you want to listen to—or not.

Be sensitive, however, about turning away when *someone has something that is important for that person to share*. It may be bad news you would prefer not to know. It may be something that will alter your experience of that person.

• Take a moment to draw strength from your Wise Being (see p 23). See if you can listen with your Wise Being's help.

Ask for a supportive visual image: a Cloak of Courage, a Robe of Compassion or a golden light which surrounds you and allows you to hear the words without them 'soaking in' (see p 206).

• Always make time to write about such a testing situation afterwards. It will 'bring out' and deepen your understanding of what was difficult. It will also give you a chance to appreciate the increased flexibility you brought to the encounter.

Speak for yourself

When two people are in conflict they may preface even more of their statements than usual with 'You . . .' followed by an accusation.

If this sounds familiar, relentlessly practise *speaking for yourself*, owning your own emotions, thoughts, attitudes, opinions.

Where accusing interchanges are part of a relationship pattern, you may want to work through this exercise with the other person involved, choosing a time when you both feel reasonably friendly, and accepting that the other person may not yet be ready to speak for her or himself. (Recognising those accusatory patterns as an avoidance of self-responsibility—and not as the last word on your inner being—will anyway reduce their sting.)

• Recall some of the accusations you have made in recent conflicts, whether these accusations were spoken aloud or hoarded silently.

Write them down so you can practise rephrasing them to speak for yourself.

Don't say 'You drive me crazy . . .' but 'I feel so angry when . . .'

Don't say 'I know you think you're better than me at this . . .' but 'I feel as though you are criticising me . . .'

Change 'You never manage a kind word for anyone . . .' to 'It makes me really sad that you seem to criticise more than praise.'

• Having written out your original and rephrased statements, try speaking the rephrased statements aloud, imagining yourself in a tense situation, but maintaining a steady sense of speaking for yourself.

It can be difficult to break old habits, and for some people it is also difficult to reach inside and know what the feelings are. But it is truly worth the effort it takes.

Understanding, not advice

Sometimes you are asked for advice, and you give what is asked for. At other times, a friend or child, co-worker, lover or spouse comes to you not for advice, but for understanding. Yet, listening to them, you are already composing your advice or even a solution.

Tuning into someone else's reality demands empathy. It also demands restraint, and the capacity to trust that the other will find relief and perhaps even clarity from your empathic listening, and will then feel able to give and take their own 'advice'.

In *You Are the World*, Krishnamurti says, 'When we talk about understanding, surely it takes place only when the mind listens completely—the mind being your heart, your nerves, your ears—when you give your whole attention to it. I do not know if you have ever noticed that when you give total attention there is complete silence.'

• Recall a situation when you were asked for understanding—and gave advice or opinions instead.

• Run the situation through in your mind again, this time visualising yourself *giving all your energy to listening*, rather than keeping most of your energy for rehearsing your advice.

• In your mind, practise checking out whether advice is wanted ('Do you want to know what I might do if I were in your shoes?').

• Practise, still in your mind, offering no advice—only support ('I can imagine how distressed/confused/hurt you must feel.').

Often the less you say the better, if this goes along with an interested, warm attitude.

• Next time understanding is asked of you, *bring your awareness to what is happening*. Let slowed-down, aware breathing help you tune in.

In the following self-therapy session, write about the encounter in your journal, checking out how you feel about the interaction and noting any small changes you still want to make.

Saying no

Crucial to intimacy is the freedom to say no without fear of reprisals. Denying yourself or someone else the right to say no expresses fear and anxiety, a confusion about your separateness and a lack of acceptance for their autonomy.

If saying no without anxiety is a consistent problem, assertiveness training will help (see p 85), but try this active meditation also. You can rehearse it in self-therapy sessions, then, when you are ready, in a real-life encounter.

• Take time to relax your body, open your mind, and acknowledge your willingness to welcome new insights.

• Think about a recent occasion when you wanted to say no, but couldn't. Or perhaps you said no, but felt so uncomfortable you might as well have said yes.

As you re-run the episode in your mind, recall your feelings and jot them down.

Be attentive to what you most feared about saying no. Write that down. 'The worse thing about saying no would have been . . .'

Now try to clarify what you were trying to save yourself—or the other person—from (anger, disappointment, rejection, scorn, dislike?).

Were there voices from the past giving you instructions how to behave in the present? Is there anything you need to say to those voices now?

• Only when you feel you have some glimmer of understanding about why you said yes in the first place, run the scene through again in your mind, this time seeing yourself say no.

How are you feeling?

If you still question your right to say no, write that down ('I want to say no but it seems too hurtful.').

• Feed that awareness directly into the situation. Rehearse how it might be for you to articulate your muddle: 'I really don't want to do this, but I am finding saying no difficult because it makes me anxious and unsure about the consequences.'

• In your following self-therapy session, recall a recent situation when someone said no to you.

Were you able to experience that without feeling attacked or rejected?

Could you say what you felt (including the conflicts)?

Did you distance yourself from what was happening to the other person (see p 185)?

• Return to saying no, and hearing no, until it feels truly comfortable for you. In the meantime, it may help to step up your affirmations of self-worth (see p 226).

Alone and together

'Even as one part of us seeks to be an individual, another part longs to restore the safety and comfort of merging with another.'

Gail Sheehy, *Passages*

It can be useful to identify those potentially conflicting desires between individuality and merging—and find ways to satisfy both.

• Relax your body and welcome the chance to get to know more deeply that part of yourself that longs for individuality or feels worn out because it is already working overtime.

Capture your feeling about individuality and allow a figure to emerge out of that feeling, as a traveller might emerge through mist. Give that subpersonality (or aspect of yourself) a descriptive name: the Adventurer, the Bold One, the Hero, Ms Capable. Write *in the first person as that subpersonality* for at least fifteen minutes, saying where you came from, what you want, in what situations you thrive, how you can help the self, where you feel valued and undervalued, and anything else that has been hidden away until now.

As you write, the subpersonality will become clearer in your mind and will probably have much to say!

• Later, perhaps in your next session, get to know the 'opposite' subpersonality that wants to merge, be protected and petted. Give her (or him) a descriptive name also: the Reed, Little One, Scared Boy, Tired Miss.

Again, write *in the first person* as that subpersonality for at least fifteen minutes. Do you (the subpersonality) feel denied, a source of shame, or overdeveloped and worn out? Are you relied on too much, or neglected?

• When you feel you have fully listened to both subpersonalities, allow them to talk to each other, saying what they want or need, and how they can work co-operatively rather than in opposition.

Take time to don your Adventurer mode. Speak to or write to the Reed, saying what you find admirable about the Reed's position (if anything); what you, the Adventurer, envy; how the Reed can help you with fresh insights, attitudes or strategies.

Now 'become' the vulnerable (or clinging?) Reed. Tell the Adventurer how you, the Reed, feel about yourself, how you experience the Adventurer: what you admire, envy, despise; what help you want.

Keep the dialogue going, speaking or writing as one subpersonality, then the other, for as long as you can.

• Later, step back a little from this dialogue. Now write in the first person as your observing self—which incorporates both these aspects or subpersonalities, and others besides.

'I notice the Adventurer wanted to . . ., but I was pulled back by . . .' 'If the subtlety of the Reed was taken up by the Adventurer, then . . .'

Formulate a resolution which incorporates one subpersonality 'borrowing' a strength from the other. Write this resolution in your journal.

• Return to this dialogue whenever you feel aspects of yourself are heading for the battlefield!

• You can also summon up the image of your Adventurer when you need a little boldness boost, and the image of your Reed when you are having difficulty accepting kindness or help.

Value the diversity of your strengths!

Attack and reconciliation

'People sometimes can't admit their caring until they have done some very painful things to one another, and someone finally cries out in agony. The process of attack and reconciliation is a mysterious one, but very powerful and ancient in human affairs.'

Carl Whitaker (with Augustus Y. Napier),
The Family Crucible

Think about just one of your intimate relationships.

• Take a recent month as an example and trace as best you can the patterns—if there are patterns—of coming together, coming apart, coming together again, coming apart.

Where there is violence in the relationship—through words,

deeds, omissions, contempt, denial, withdrawal, attack—see if there is a pattern there too: what precedes what; what follows what?

Where there is violence, take as much time as you need to explore the questions that follow. Start with just one at a time, perhaps the one that seems to fit your situation most closely. Go inside with your eyes closed and hold the question in your mind. As thoughts and feelings arise, write them down, then continue to go back inside, then write; withdraw, write, for at least fifteen minutes. Give yourself at least another fifteen minutes to muse on what you have written, no matter how sparse or unsatisfactory. Sometimes a fragment is all you need to shift you to a different level of understanding.

What is the history of violence in my life?

What feeds the violence in my life now?

Do I feel fated to be violent, or to be in the presence of violence?

Do I feel compelled to return to a violent situation to rewrite an old ending?

What is the violence asking for (see dream dialogue, p 44)?

What rewards do I get for or from the violence (see p 189)?

Where there are rewards, how could I get those without the violence?

If I currently feel powerless to contain the violence in myself, am I willing to work with that issue (see pp 173, 194, 195)?

If I feel powerless to stop the violence of another person, can I act with self-love to get the help and support I fully deserve?

VIOLENCE IS ALWAYS AN ASSAULT ON YOUR DEEPEST SENSE OF SELF, AND YOUR CAPACITY FOR SELF-LOVE.

There is never an adequate excuse for violence.

Refusing negative projections

Cynicism, contempt, prejudice, judgement, hostility, belittlement, hatred, envy, sarcasm: these are the enemies of self-love and love for others.

It is not possible to separate or protect yourself from the negative emotions you express towards other people. It is, however, possible for you to refuse to 'take on' or 'take in' the negative emotions other people express towards you.

• Use a self-therapy session to rehearse the following steps until they feel real to you. *See yourself* acting self-protectively. *Experience* how empowering that feels. If you feel forced to work or live in an excessively competitive or hostile environment, these steps can provide you with the armour you need.

1 In the face of someone else's contempt or hostility, take an imaginative step backwards, remembering that the person is expressing *their worldview* and describing *how they are feeling*. This may be far from an accurate portrayal of you. *Slow and deepen your breathing*.

2 Imaginatively surround yourself with a tent or cone of bright golden light. Through this golden light you can see the person and hear everything they are saying, but their words cannot penetrate you. You can shake them off as a duck shakes water from its back. *Continue to slow and deepen your breathing*.

• When such an attack happens in real life, use your awareness of your slowed breath to recall those two simple steps.

Review the incident later to see if the strategy worked for you. Do you need to rehearse it again?

• When such an attack arouses your self-hatred, or lifts your anxiety levels, breathe deeply and slowly: *wrap yourself in love*.

Avoiding suspicion

Here is a way to identify an aspect of yourself that may be causing you problems. By working with this subpersonality (or aspect of yourself), you can discover that in any situation you have a breadth of responses available. Remind yourself who is choosing!

• Take several minutes for each of the following questions, jotting down your first reaction and then your more considered reaction to each.

Is your general attitude towards people defensive, wary or suspicious?

Do you expect other people to try to take advantage of you?

Do you feel vulnerable to attack?

If you hear even a reluctant yes, then the subpersonality or aspect of yourself you could call the Persecuted One needs to be acknowledged—and maybe retired.

Remember, the Persecuted One became part of your emotional repertoire for sound reasons. Perhaps disappointment and pain did once dominate your life, and now the Persecuted One is still trying to save you from disappointment by spoiling encounters even before they happen.

When such a potential encounter is looming—and suspicious thoughts are revving up in a familiar way—rehearse the following strategy.

• Use your awareness as your ally.

Recognise the voice of your Persecuted One ('She will never give me a chance . . .'; 'He wants to ruin my presentation . . .'; 'They never want to give me any credit . . .'). Know the voice for what it is: an out-of-date attempt to protect you that may not bear any relation to this current person's attitude or intention.

• Acknowledge what is happening. Writing it down will help.

'I'm hearing the voice of my Persecuted One. She thinks she's warning me. I can hear her saying . . .'

• Write down how you intend this situation to be different.

'I will leave the Persecuted One outside the room. I will take as much time as I need to see how this situation, in the present, unfolds. I will keep an open mind.'

• There may be another subpersonality you could present in potentially loaded encounters.

Take time to go into your inner world, and ask another bolder and more optimistic aspect of yourself to come forward. Give that aspect a name: the Curious One, the Big Smiler, the See-Saw Champ (always in balance!). Have fun with that process of naming.

Promise to get to know that aspect better by writing to it, talking to it, making friends with it, finding out what it can do for you.

• The Persecuted One's attitudes may persist. Don't brush them away. Write them down fully. When you feel written out, acknowledge the help the Persecuted One was trying to give, but remind yourself there are more positive approaches to adopt.

In a single sentence, formulate your positive approach.

'I want this encounter to be optimistic and will have the Big Smiler on my side.'

• If the Persecuted One is proved right—you were not given a chance; you were cheated and disappointed—see that outcome for what it is: a disappointment in the present, not a pointer to a string of disappointments in the future, and not a reason to revert to a self-defeating stance that poses as self-protection.

When is a relationship over?

Individual desires and levels of tolerance vary greatly.

It is virtually impossible for anyone outside a relationship to say when two people have had enough and would benefit more from parting, even with sadness and loss, than they would from persisting in their connection and using their difficulties as a chance to learn and grow.

But when it has been a sexual relationship and the two people are no longer lovers, *and at least one of them feels unhappy about that*, it may be healthier and more truthful to shift the relationship into a friendship, when that is appropriate, or to separate more decidedly until the inevitable pain of loss, the hurts and disappointments have been worked through.

When attempting to unravel a big change of this kind it is always useful to use the basic tools of self-discovery: meditation, drawing, writing, dreaming.

It is also vital to remember that often we feel forced into making a decision—any decision—because we cannot tolerate a state of 'not knowing'. Yet time itself can offer solutions; and often does.

• Using any or all of those means to focus your awareness, you might consider the following questions. Take your time with each one of them. They may carry you through several self-therapy sessions.

Am I largely connected to my partner out of my strength or my weakness?

Does being with my partner bring out the best in me most of the time?

Do I feel alive in this relationship?

Do I feel alive in my head as well as my body; in my soul as well as my heart?

Do I feel easier or more alive when my partner is not around?

Am I growing within this relationship?

Are there important aspects of myself I keep hidden from my partner?

Can I share what means most to me with this person?

What am I expecting this person to bring to me that he or she is not?

Are my expectations realistic?

Am I considering leaving at the same point in this relationship as I left any other relationship which preceded it?

Has my partner failed to make up for my own feelings of emptiness?

How do I feel when I imagine life without my partner?

Have I used my creativity to identify where change is needed?

Am I willing to make changes in myself?

Would I prefer to shift my attitudes and responses within the relationship, rather than ending the relationship itself?

Do I persist with the relationship because my partner has qualities or strengths I need to develop in myself?

If I decide to stay, or to leave, then who am I primarily pleasing?

Am I willing to strengthen my relationship with my own self whether or not I stay with my partner?

- Return often to the questions which resonate with you. You may also want to spend self-therapy time meditating on the self of the other (see p 159) and exploring what matters most to you (see pp 112, 161).

This is a time to be awake and aware.

Separating—and learning

When one or both people in a couple feel ambivalent about being together, or when there is a sense of pulling apart rather than coming towards, then the question inevitably arises: 'Should we separate?'

Whether this is a casual question or life-shaking often depends on how long the two people have been together, what other people are involved—especially dependent children—whether the two people have the psychological strength and the financial means to separate. It may also depend on whether one person feels the other is acting as decision-maker, leaving their partner with uncomfortable feelings of frustration and powerlessness.

The way in which two people part will often mirror, almost uncannily, the way they conducted their relationship. The pain of parting in all relationships—gay or heterosexual—will resonate with other power struggles as well as losses from the past. In heterosexual relationships, there may also be the frustrations and fury that can accompany gender-stereotyped behaviours. If the woman habitually 'carried' and even expressed the feelings for both partners, she will do so during the time of separation also. If the man sought solace or distraction elsewhere during the relationship, he will probably do so during the separation. If the woman habitually directs passively, then she will push him to act as though he were leaving her. If his pain is usually expressed as rage, there are likely to be huge scenes at this time. If her fear of loss is expressed in clinging, manipulative behaviour, then so she will struggle to the end. If she usually talks and he usually fails to listen, then so it will be in the final scenes.

Only a willingness to learn from the experience of separation can change those patterns.

Parting with awareness rather than with denial; parting with sorrow rather than anger; increasing attention to self-responsibility rather than blaming; acknowledging the loss of what could not be; using the upheaval of change for self-discovery and growth: those would be the best possible preparations for the almost universal hope when two people part—that next time it will be different.

If you are facing a separation or possible separation you could usefully spend several sessions returning to this same exploration.

• Take time to slow down and consider what this parting means to you. Free Writing (see p 32) will help. You could take as your guiding sentence 'Without this relationship I am . . .' or 'Changing this relationship I feel . . .'

It will help to ask your inner world for an image for the way you feel about what is happening right now. Draw the image. Ask the image what it has to tell you (see p 31).

• Become more aware about the way you want to part, and how you will accept your partner's decision.

List all the emotions and thoughts and contradictions that accompany this parting. Having put them all down, you might decide that there are several rocky areas you will attend to in forthcoming self-therapy sessions, and there is one thought you will take as your guide. Formulate that into a sentence which expresses your willingness to be conscious of what's happening in this time of change ('I accept that I have no sexual partner at present and am choosing not to have casual sex.'). Note it in your journal.

• Decide what your crucial next step will be: both in relation to your former partner, and to yourself as a now-unpartnered person.

Formulate that, too, into a sentence and note it in your journal.

• When negotiating the separation, hone your listening skills (see p 196) and practise speaking for yourself (see p 200). That will stand you in good stead at a time when you may feel unusually fragile.

• If anger colours your interactions, let some of that anger go (see p 195). It may be preventing you from feeling loss, pain and disappointment. Those are painful emotions, but can be survived.
• Ask your Wise Being (see p 23) for what you need so you can be true to yourself *at each small, next step*.

How to avoid fights!

What follows looks suspiciously like a recipe. (I hate psychological recipes!) But in this case, have fun with it. Avoid fights with it. Take time to write down your reactions to it in your journal. Note your resistances to change and understand what rewards you might be getting from fighting.

Unusually, talk with your nearest and dearest about the principles which lie behind this approach to not-fighting. Discover what you yourself feel about fighting as you assess your reactions when others agree or disagree with what you're saying. ('Fights need to happen.' 'Fights can be avoided and the issues dealt with some other way.' 'Every couple fights—let's have it out in the open.')

• Take two people.
• Add a busy day, massive pollution, perhaps a pinch of crying children, a teaspoonful of dog's barking, and a handful of telephone rings.
• Drop by drop, stir in a cupful of anxiety from the past, and mix thoroughly. Put on stove. Turn to high.
• *As soon as* the mixture gets to boiling point, take off the stove.
• Do not let the mixture boil for a second longer than it should. It is crucial to attend to a fight mixture before it gets out of control, and not after.
• Separate the two people from the rest of the mixture.
• Cool them down, briefly.

• If they feel they must speak, ask them each to speak for themselves, to describe *only* their own thoughts and feelings and *always* in the first person.

• Do not allow them to attack or criticise the other person, nor tell that other person any single thing that is 'for their own good'.

• Sprinkle icing sugar over whatever cracks have developed in the mixture.

• Where necessary, they should be willing to eat their words.

PART FIVE

Desire

'There is something I have noticed about desire, that it opens the eyes and strikes them blind at the same time.'

Jane Smiley, *The Age of Grief*

Introduction

Moving through this final section of the *Self-Therapy Book* you will, with increasing ease, find you can accept that life is not always going to give what you want. *And it may not always matter*. You may discover familiar patterns of needing and wanting are dissolving as less stereotyped and more personal possibilities arise from within.

Seeking warmth, contact, appreciation, and the satisfactions of feeling understood, it can be liberating to experience that to desire is not only to desire sexually and that to love is not only to focus on a single relationship. You can be loving—and feel the energising power of eros—in the way you breathe, the way you speak, the way you listen; you can be loving through your increased awareness of others; you can be loving in the way you meet another person's gaze, and answer their smile with your own.

Experiencing love, feeling love as the energy which fuels your life, you can turn inwards with satisfaction to a whole variety of intimate relationships, and you can turn outwards also—trusting your own self and your loved ones to survive while you simultaneously discover where your life connects with the world beyond your immediate concerns.

To allow your desiring to tell you more about who you are and what you seek, you need time for dreaming and for listening. It is listening to your inner world that can take you from stunted, repetitive cries of 'I want' to a more inclusive experience of desiring and an enriched experience of having. Reaching out, searching 'out there' for the ideal person, relationship, political cause or spiritual teacher, you can fail to experience what is happening, now, as you wait for the bus, as you bend to tie your child's shoes, as you lift a hand—to protest or caress.

Without going out of my door
I can know all things on earth.
Without looking out of my window
I can know the ways of heaven.

For the further one travels
The less one knows.

The sage therefore
Arrives without travelling,
Sees all without looking,
Does all without doing.

> Lao Tzu, *Tao Te Ching*,
> Verse 47

In the eyes of my ideal lover, I am . . .

Perhaps you would want the ideal lover to experience you as, at the very least
    kind
    beautiful
    serene
    creative
    forgiving
    lovable
    wise
    funny.

• Spend a delightful half hour or so choosing the qualities you would most wish to be appreciated for; the qualities you want to colour your life.

When you have finished, take time to select three or four you want most.

• Write the names of those qualities on cards. Decorate them as beautifully as you can. Place the cards around your rooms at home, or in your workplace.

• Meditate on those qualities by bringing them repeatedly to your awareness. Open your mind and heart to the varied ways they can be expressed.

Where you want extra support, borrow the behaviour you need (see p 62).

• Acknowledge and appreciate those qualities in others.

Meditation on love (1)

Driving much of your desiring will be your longing and need for love.

I use this meditation often, both alone and working with others. It never fails to lift my spirits and return my focus to what matters.

It is a version of one of the most popular discursive meditations practised by Theravadin Buddhists. They recommend it be recited in the morning to create a mood of love and compassion for the rest of the day. I cannot endorse that practice strongly enough. The meditation has the power of transformation in every word.

• Read it aloud, or put it onto a tape so you can sit quietly and absorb it.

My mind is at this moment pure, free from all impurities;
free from lust, hatred and ignorance;
free from all evil thoughts.

My mind is pure and clean. Like a polished mirror
is my stain-free mind.

*As a clean and empty vessel is filled with pure water, so I now fill my
clean heart and pure mind with peaceful and sublime thoughts of
boundless love, overflowing compassion, empathy, joy and perfect peace.*

*I have now washed my mind and my heart free of anger,
ill-will, cruelty, violence, jealousy, envy, passion and aversion.*

*May I be well and happy!
May I be free from suffering, disease, grief, worry and anger!
May I be strong, self-confident, healthy and peaceful!*

*Now I am bringing to every particle of my system, from my head to my feet,
thoughts of boundless love and compassion.
I embody love and compassion.
My whole body is saturated with love and compassion.
I am a stronghold, a fortress of love and compassion.*

What I have, I now give to others.

*My mind turns to those people I know best. I think of them,
individually and collectively.
I fill them with thoughts of loving kindness.
I wish them peace and happiness.
Again and again I say:* May all beings be well and be happy.

*My mind turns to all seen and unseen beings, living near and far:
women, men, animals and all living creatures, in the East, West,
North, South, above and below.
I radiate to them boundless loving kindness, without any enmity or
obstruction.
I radiate loving kindness to all, irrespective of class, creed, colour or sex.*

*Those people are all my sisters and brothers, fellow-beings in the ocean of
life.
I identify with them all.
I am one with them all.
Ten times I will say:*
May they all be well and happy . . .
I wish them, as much as myself, all peace and happiness.

Meditation on love (2)

This tiny meditation is crucial to my wellbeing. I practise it, teach it, urge it on others. I am even tempted to suggest that if you use nothing else from this book on a regular basis that you make this meditation your own. *Surround yourself with love.*

- Calm your mind, slow your breathing.
  Your mind is focused only on your breathing: in, out; in, out.
  When you are ready, on the in-breath, begin to take in peace.
  Take it from the environment, from the earth, from trees, from the air you are breathing in.
  On the out-breath, breathe out love.
  Surround yourself with love.

That is all: breathe in peace, breathe out love.

As the meditation continues, go on taking in peace and breathing out love but you may wish, sometimes, to send this love outwards in ever-enlarging circles.

You can also choose to alter the first word: breathing in generosity, trust, serenity, acceptance. Take what you need. Breathe out love.

From fear to love

It is possible to transform the energy of fear into that of love.

This exercise can be done slowly as you learn it, and then almost instantly.

- Clench and unclench your fists while you breathe deeply. Shake your arms, and your hands, vigorously. Shake your legs vigorously, your feet, perhaps your whole body: shoulders, hips, head. *Shake.*

- When you have shaken away your excess energy, shift your consciousness away from your body, away from your feelings, away from your mind. You are giving yourself a welcome break from your own attention!

• Visualise something beautiful. It might be a rainbow, a star. It might be the steady flame of a candle or a white light.

• When you have that image steady in your mind's eye, allow the energy from that rainbow, star, candle or white light to move towards you and enter you.

This is the energy of love.

Let that love flow through you and settle into you.

Be greedy. There is no limit to the amount of love you can take in.

As thoughts come into your mind, allow them to drift by. Then turn your attention back to the energy of love.

• Keep your focus on the source of the love still flowing into your body.

• Only when you feel ready to do so, open your eyes and move back into your everyday life, knowing that you have been filled with love.

You can return to that source of love as often as you wish with no greater effort than closing your eyes and summoning up the image that brought love to you.

Focus on the present

Desiring, you hurtle yourself into the future, looking to a time when you will have what you don't have now. In small doses, this can be fine. But it is also important to be aware of what is happening, and what you have, *at this moment*.

All your self-therapy will, one way or another, support your capacity to be alive in the present moment, but here is a way to give this crucial issue extra attention. As a goal-driven person (always with projects to finish, projects coming up, deadlines to meet), I find living in the present a major challenge. I am only too aware how my rhetoric outstrips my practice. But every time I do make a small step forward, the benefits show in every aspect of my life but nowhere more so than in my most personal relationships, with my children and with my own self.

Be here now. I use that expression often. It doesn't mean I don't sail away again. But there's no limit to the times I can embrace those words, *Be here now*, and allow them to work their easeful magic.

• Take time to observe your thoughts over several days, and become more familiar with your own patterns. Watching your thoughts (see p 41) will help. Note down what you observe in your journal. Note *patterns of thinking* rather than the thoughts themselves.

Are your thoughts often in the past, or pitched ahead into the future?

Are you always *about to become a better person*, rather than appreciating who you are now? (This is true of my clients; I notice it again and again.)

Are your thoughts often with people *other than those in the room with you, right now*?

Are your thoughts often on projects *other than the one you are doing right now*?

• Bring yourself into the present at regular intervals (see p 255).
• In your next self-therapy session, return to your patterns of thinking to discover how much of your anxiety relates to what might happen—but is not happening at this very moment.

It cannot help you to worry about *what might never happen*. Visualise how much lighter you will feel when you are no longer worrying about hypothetical issues.

Unburden yourself. Make that resolution specific. Write down a practical change in attitude in your journal. Monitor your progress positively and self-supportingly.

Trust

Desiring—even hoping—may seem impossible when your capacity to trust yourself and others has run dry. It is possible to learn to trust, but in small stages only, and starting with your own self.

• Create an affirmation of self-trust. Here is an example. Write your own from observations drawn from within yourself, and from your immediate environment.

I am alive. I trust that.

I have a body. I trust that.

I can feel. I trust that.

I can think. I trust that.

When my hand brushes across my face, I can trust that.

I can breathe in the air that surrounds me. I can trust that.

I can smell the perfume of flowers. I can trust that.

When I dive into the ocean I feel the aliveness of the waves. I can trust that.

• Encourage your affirmation to grow. Read or sing it out loud once or twice each day. Don't hesitate to add something absurd ('My dog has fleas. I can trust that.') or perhaps something painful ('My parents are dead. I can trust that.').

Over time, choose to appreciate that what you are trusting about yourself and your environment is growing, and is allowing you to trust a little more deeply and broadly.

• Only when you are ready, begin to add what you can trust about other people. Again, don't hesitate to add absurd observations to more serious ones.

• While you are giving attention to this issue of trust, you may want to meditate on the qualities you need (see p 145). Make cards which blazen COURAGE, HOPE, TRUST. Let those cards work for you.

You may also feel supported by learning how to transform the energy of fear into that of love (see p 221).

Who is in charge of your life?

'. . . every time you make a choice you are turning the central part of you, the part of you that chooses, into something a little different from what it was before. And taking your life as a whole, with all your innumerable choices, all your life you are slowly turning this central thing into either a heavenly creature or into a hellish creature.'

C. S. Lewis, *Mere Christianity*

Desiring, you may send out a message that someone else carries the key to your happiness in the palm of their hand. Despairing, you may blame others for the way your life is today.

Take back your power.

Use Free Drawing (see p 30) to explore what obstacles lie between who you are at this moment and who you would need to be to feel at ease in your inner world, and responsible for the world you create around you.

Take your time with all aspects of this exploration and return as often as you want to the steps of drawing, dialoguing, speaking to your Wise Being, identifying needed strengths and resolving to 'borrow' them until they become unselfconsciously your own.

• Draw an image or a series of images for yourself as the person who feels that family, fate, chance or convention, or someone who is stronger than you are, is in charge of your life.

You may want to draw one image for your own self and another image for whoever or whatever has more power in your life than you do.

When you feel confident you have drawn all you can, patiently speak to the image or images you have drawn (see p 31), asking it or them to tell you what needs to shift or change before you can feel confident that you are in charge of your own life and at peace within it.

Write down whatever 'message' you get, no matter how tentative or fragmentary.

The message may be another image. If so, draw that without immediately worrying if you understand it. Whatever its current, life-based associations are for you will bring you new insights and information.

• Ask your Wise Being (see p 23) to help you further identify what would allow you to feel in charge of your own life.

Close your eyes, bring to mind the face of your Wise Being, address your question and wait patiently. If there is no immediate answer, trust that this will come soon, now that you have awakened your inner world to your need for guidance.

Julianna was an abused child. Having painfully recognised how tormenting this was, she wrote, 'I have to resist the strident voice that tells me I deserve to be treated badly and I have to resist the feeling I have of "being at home" in a tense, punitive situation. I can use my awareness to resist this at least sometimes. I'm also practising the affirmations of self-worth and love to provide a different, self-chosen chorus to run in my head.'

• Bring to mind an image of someone you believe has their life together. What qualities do you perceive that person has? Feel free to borrow those qualities until they are yours (see p 62) and also meditate on them (see pp 145, 146).

An affirmation of self-worth

Are you desiring nurturance and dreaming of love, yet find yourself being put down, ignored or denigrated?

Is there a voice in your own mind that questions whether you deserve any better and mocks your capacity to hope?

• You cannot always change the voices outside yourself, but you can increase the sense of self-worth that sustains you from within. The following affirmation can be whispered, shouted, spoken or sung. Change it and expand it to suit your wildest dreams! Use all of it or just a memorised line or two whenever you feel assaulted by your own self-doubts, or the violence or unhappiness of another human being.

Limit your willingness to be a repository for someone else's psychic pain.
Be clear what you can bear. Beyond that point, seek help.

I am a human being, worthy of gentleness.
I am a human being, worthy of respect.
I am a human being, worthy of touch.
I am a human being, worthy of consideration.
I am a human being, worthy of being listened to.
I am a human being, worthy of love.
I am a human being, worthy of laughter.
I am a human being, worthy of caring.
I am a human being, worthy of trust.
I am a human being, worthy of peace.

What's missing?

This quest to discover what is missing from your life will not lead to self-pity. It may give you some clarity about how your present life is affected by your past. It may also give you the chance to mourn or rage when that's necessary. It may allow you to understand better why you feel empty even when you get what you thought you most wanted. The meditation can be done often, with new insights gradually emerging at ever-deeper levels of your consciousness.

• Take ten pieces of card or paper.
 Write, on each, something that is missing from your life.
 Move inwards as you write, so that initially you might note that you are missing the car you want, and finally you may note that the child in you is still missing being taken seriously. Write without censorship or judgement.
• When you have finished put the cards in two piles.
 On one pile, place the cards describing missing things that you

think can be realised (perhaps in an unexpected or more creative way than you have so far contemplated).

On the other, place the cards describing things gone for ever, things that cannot be replaced, or of significant loss.

• Take your time to explore each card individually.

Use drawing, writing, dreaming, drifting and self-questioning, jotting down whatever comes to mind, however apparently obscure or irrelevant.

• When you return to the cards that have some potential, welcome the chance to think about what is missing as a challenge and not a problem only. Be patient, and alert. You may want to formulate a request and take it to your Wise Being (see p 23), without expecting an immediate or predictable response.

'I am missing courage to develop my intellectual life. I need help.'

'I am missing the feeling side of my personality. I need help.'

'I miss having a job and feeling useful. I need help.'

'I miss my ex-lover constantly. I need help.'

• When you work with the cards where what is missing has gone forever, you will probably uncover feelings of deprivation, grief or desperation. Honour those feelings. Don't rush past them. It may be appropriate to talk about them to a friend. If you do not have such a person in your life, use your journal as your confidante, or turn to the compassionate understanding of your Wise Being, again asking for help, and accepting that it may come in an unpredictable way.

'I am bringing you my sadness that my partner is dead. I need help.'

'I am bringing you my desperation that I am paralysed. I need help.'

'I am bringing you my rage that I didn't get what every child deserves. I need help.'

• Stay with your pain and your questions, perhaps intensifying your experience by returning to Facing the impossible (see p 137), or Loss and grief (see p 119). But also take in the love you need, stepping up your practice of the meditations on love (see pp 219, 221), no matter how hollow the words may sometimes feel.

Life is unfair

Life is unfair.

Your boss is unfair.

The universe is unfair.

God is unfair.

Your wage packet is unfair.

Your living conditions are unfair.

Your spotty face/fat thighs/straggly hair are unfair.

It is unfair that you are so old/young/sick/unhappily married/alone.

• Make yourself comfortable. Take a few deep breaths to clear away tensions. Relax your belly, your hands, feet, tongue, chin. (Is there anywhere else that needs a moment's attention?)

• List as many 'unfairnesses' as you can. You may need several sheets of paper. Withdraw into yourself to muse on this issue, then jot down your thoughts and feelings; withdraw, write; withdraw, write. If you notice any tensions creeping back into your body as you write, note those.

Read over your list, and then ask yourself if you surely couldn't find a few more items to add. Add them!

• When you have emptied yourself, consider how dominating—and prophetic—those 'unfair' thoughts can be. You may want to write down your reactions to that thought, and perhaps even stop here until your next self-therapy session.

• Circle those which seem to carry most energy, or are felt by you most persistently, and explore those major 'unfairnesses' one at a time. Jot down all your associations with them.

Are they unfairnesses from the past, or in the present?

Do current unfairnesses feel especially oppressive because of past associations (a drug-abusing partner when you had an alcohol-abusing parent)?

Are they unfairnesses that affect the way you think, or feel?

Do they batter at your self-esteem, or affect your attitudes towards others, or perhaps about life itself?

Spend as much time as you need writing, thinking, drawing, dreaming. Take at least fifteen minutes to write and a further fifteen minutes to muse, and add additional thoughts.

• When you understand the history of those unfairnesses, as well as having a sense of their current power, ask yourself if you are ready to make a modest resolution.

If you are, resolve to take some small but crucial action, *knowing this will be empowering*. Write down your resolution in your journal where you can monitor it and support yourself.

'My wage is unfair. I will use my anger and get involved with the union.'

'It's unfair I was sexually abused. I will find the self-help group I need.'

'It is unfair I had such cold and unloving parents. I am clear I will be a very different kind of person and will refuse their example with all my strength.'

• Perhaps the challenge for you is not to take action, but to practise acceptance. This can be deeply challenging.

A first step may be to formulate that acceptance and write it down.

'It is unfair I'm without paid work at fifty. I will accept it, not because I want to but so it won't pollute my whole life.'

'It's unfair I won't have any children. I will allow myself to grieve, and get help with that.'

• Accepting what is unfair *but can't be changed* will allow you to get on with whatever else is happening in your life—or could happen.

Feelings of unfairness translate rapidly into envy and anger. While your attention is held by what is unfair, you cannot develop your awareness of what is potentially or actually nourishing in your life—and have more of that.

• When a sense of unfairness persists, or clings as self-pity, *acknowledge it*. Only then, turn your attention *consciously* to what you can be grateful for. Write those things down. Don't let them escape, no matter how apparently trivial.

'I have food to cook. I had a perfect orange today. I heard some music that made me remember my friend Amanda. I laughed when my son told me the joke about the three-legged dog . . .'

Asking for what you want

Feeling safe to ask for what you want, *and knowing you can tolerate the other person saying no*, is crucial to an easy relationship with your own self, as well as to the success of any intimate connection. It makes things clear between people and downplays the need to second-guess, which depletes many relationships and rarely leads to either person having their needs met.

Here is a loud, uninhibited exercise which is a first step towards feeling that it is fine to ask for what you want, and that it will also (eventually) be all right not always to get it!

Unless you are exceptionally unselfconscious, try this when you are alone at home or in an open space away from other people. Have your journal and a pen handy, and some paper and crayons.

• Decide what you want to ask for. Do not censor this asking: go for it.

    'I want Catherine to love me.'

    'I want to love myself.'

    'I want to lose twenty pounds.'

    'I want to save the rainforests.'

    'I want someone else to take care of me.'

    'I want to stop feeling depressed.'

    'I want a job.'

    'I want to be well.'

• Ask for it again.

• Ask for it slowly.

• Ask for it fast.

• Ask for it loud, louder, loudest.

• Shout it out.

• Scream it out.

• Shout and stamp. Shout, shake or moan.

• Be filled with nothing but your 'I want'.

• When you have asked to the full capacity of your being, ask again! And again.

• If your pulse is not racing, if you are not hot, sweaty and laughing (or crying) you need more! On you go, *you want it*.

• When you feel puffed, hoarse and replete, rest a while. Then, when you are ready, jot down whatever comes to your mind—anything at all, no matter how apparently disconnected from what you have just been asking for. If you feel like drawing instead of writing, or as well as, then you should do what you want!

• As you sit writing about your experience, old habits of thought and attitude may tell you, 'You can't have what you want,' or, 'You never get what you want.' Remind those habits of the energy and heat of your wanting—and tell them times are changing! Some of what you want is what you are going to have *even if you shouldn't; even if you are truly undeserving*.

Your hands are open.

Not getting what you want

Little children who don't get what they want, at the moment they want it and in just the way they want it, will often lie on the ground and scream. Sometimes adults react similarly! Yet you cannot always judge an ideal outcome at the moment of obsessive desiring.

Sometimes not getting what you want may save misery later on.

Sometimes not getting what you want leaves you available to get something more rewarding a little later.

Sometimes not getting what you want—and accepting that is part of life—*is all that is happening*.

• Disappointment is part of life. *Conscious* acceptance of that, and a willingness to withstand disappointment, can give you comfort and emotional flexibility.

I won't always get what I want. I can bear that.

Write those lines down a few times, or say them aloud. As you write, note what feelings come up—and how convinced you feel.

If you are not entirely convinced, familiarise yourself with the feelings that accompany disappointment. It will help to focus on a recent situation, observing the powerlessness, rage, sulking, denial, manipulation or longing for revenge that may be your habitual response to disappointment.

Do those feelings 'belong' to this particular situation? Or are they a global response from the past: 'I never get what I want.'

• Run that same situation through your mind again, now with this thought in mind: *I won't always get what I want. I can bear that.*

Spend at least fifteen minutes with that thought. Jot down your reactions; withdraw to muse; write, withdraw. Notice when your breathing is shallow or tense.

It may take some time to convince the pessimistic part of yourself that you can bear disappointment more flexibly. Ask your Wise Being (see p 23) for an image or talisman to inspire you.

• In *A Conscious Person's Guide to Relationships*, Ken Keyes Jr encourages a switch from addictive thinking ('I have to have this outcome.') to a state of mind where a *preference* is acknowledged ('I would like this outcome most.'). A preference allows you to be open to a variety of outcomes, and not addicted to one only. It is a switch of thinking that can work fast and effectively (see p 238).

Simply keep in mind: *I would prefer this outcome; I am not addicted to it.*

Refusing others what they want

There is a fine line between making yourself too readily available to others (assuming they can't take care of themselves or that you can take care of them better) and withholding what would make life a little more comfortable for others. Either of those situations provides a clue that all is not well with the self: the self you can trust to be generous; the self you can trust to be respectful of others.

You might, for example, be consistently unreliable.

You might habitually keep others waiting.

Perhaps you are not available to other people when they have legitimate requests—*unless it suits you*.

Perhaps you regard all requests for your time as intrusive or demanding.

This pattern describes many people in personal and business situations where there are hierarchical boundaries to affirm one person's right to deny others' requests or needs. That may seem like an exercise of power, but it is equally possible (and arguably more accurate) to see it as an example of powerlessness, for when you are on 'secure ground inside yourself'—to quote Marie-Louise von Franz—there will be enough 'self' to acknowledge the legitimacy of others' needs, even when it is not always possible to meet them.

• Use a self-therapy session (or several) to explore the questions that follow. With all these questions test your theoretical response ('This is what I believe I do.') against recent practical experiences ('This is what I actually did.'). Hold each question in your mind. See yourself acting and reacting. Jot down your thoughts and feelings. Move slowly, taking at least five to ten minutes for each question: thinking, writing; withdrawing, writing.

When is it possible for me to put myself into someone else's shoes and imagine what they are feeling?

In what situations do I allow myself to be sensitive to others' feelings (home, work, with 'superiors', 'inferiors', those like me, those unlike me)?

When is it difficult to act on my awareness that other people's feelings or needs may differ from mine and still be legitimate?

Do I find it hard to believe my behaviour affects other people? Am I willing to *act as if* my behaviour affects others, until experience gives me a fresh perspective?

Do I sometimes boost my ego by putting people down, keeping them waiting, belittling them, letting them know how important I am? Are there other ways I can tend to my self, rather than boosting my ego?

Are there situations when I choose to be so efficient/busy/important that I justify disrespect to others? How could I change that?

If I put myself in the place of those with whom I am interacting, would I feel happy with my responses and behaviour?

How could I change my tactics or habitual responses when that seems called for?

What changes do I need to make *in the way I experience myself* so that I can be respectful to others in all situations, including business?

• Only when you feel you have explored each question fully, using recent situations as your guide, should you decide on a small but significant change you are willing to make.

This change should express your increased awareness of others.

Write that resolution as a single, simple sentence in your journal. Review it regularly. Make sure that your self-development takes place in every area of your life, and that you are not beauty in one arena, and the beast in another!

Moving from wanting to needing

Behind most wanting lie needs, sometimes pining for lack of recognition, or silenced by the clamorous cry of 'I want ...' Understanding those needs does not mean they will necessarily be satisfied, but a need is generally more flexible than a want, and is more likely to be met from resources within yourself or your environment.

• On a large sheet or several sheets of paper write 'I want ...' until you feel completely emptied out. Don't just list what you want. Each time, write in full 'I want ...' whatever it is.

Take a few minutes break. Breathe deeply, or shake yourself free of excess energy. Look at what you have written. Can that be all? Write on.

A typical list will include sensible things ('I want to be less grumpy with my partner's children.' 'I want to find a satisfying job.'); utopian things ('I want a year in Tahiti.'); impossible things ('I want to be perfect.').

• When you feel ready, choose three items from your list that are more urgent 'wants' than the rest. Take your time choosing.

• Use Free Writing (see p 32) to explore those wants, using as your guiding sentence: 'I want . . . because . . .'

You may need to write this same sentence many times before you push through your most immediate thoughts or feelings to a deeper level.

• Move on to consider your needs.

Perhaps while writing down your wants, the needs that lie behind them have already spilled onto the page.

'I want a job because I need the money.'

'I want a job because I need to be useful.'

Patiently explore and identify all the needs which may lie behind a particular want. Write them down; withdrawing to ponder, writing; withdrawing, writing.

• Consider which of those needs seem paramount and can realistically be met, given your circumstances and environment. Here you will want to be both creative and realistic. It is useful to remember that *the more abstract a need is, the more easily it can be met.* ('I need Alex to love me' is tricky to satisfy if Alex cannot love you. 'I need love' can be addressed in many ways.)

• Ask yourself, 'Is someone else required to meet my need, or could I bring into my life the qualities I associate with the need all by myself?'

Paula gave a lovely response when answering that question. She has a much older husband, and step-children who are in late middle age. Paula said, 'I moved from wanting to be twenty-nine again—which is not easy at forty-five—to needing to seem young, to needing to feel young, to needing to be around younger people! I think I can manage that.'

• Make a modest resolution about how you can honour and meet at least one of your needs. Promise yourself time and energy to review regularly what your needs are and how you can use your creativity to meet them.

Wants and needs in conflict

Perhaps you and a friend, colleague or partner each wants something you feel entitled to have, but your wants seem incompatible.

Here is a way to ease a potentially painful situation.

• Each person needs time to locate the particular want that feels urgent. Focus it so that it can be described in a single sentence. Write that down: 'I want . . .'

• Now take at least fifteen minutes to think *through* or beyond your 'wanting' to the need that lies behind it.

You may want to try writing out a whole number of needs before one strikes you as having more force than the rest. (You can use your Magic Wand [see p 28] to explore the need, should it elude you.)

• Now you have two focused statements. They might resemble these:

'I want your reassurances. *I need to know you won't leave me.*'

'I want you to stop harassing me. *I need my feeling of freedom.*'

'I want you to work in a more co-operative way. *I need our partnership to continue.*'

• Recognising each other's *needs* is all this particular exercise asks of you.

Often having a need recognised and brought into the open relieves as much tension as if the need itself is met. You don't believe me? Try it! Our drive to be understood is strong.

• When a solution has to be found beyond the simple recognition of needs, it is easier to do this satisfactorily for all concerned when you transform your erstwhile opponent into an ally. That is, the two people focus *jointly* on those needs, bringing their creativity and flexibility to A's needs, and then to B's needs.

For people who are frequently in conflict, this can be an immensely powerful and liberating way to negotiate.

Filling the sky with hot-air balloons

You will rarely manage to guarantee a desired outcome by worrying, yet when things matter most, anxiety may dominate your entire experience. Setting that anxiety aside *by refusing to be single-minded about the outcome* can be hugely liberating. Here's how to try it.

• Select a recent or current situation where a single desirable outcome is fixed in your mind. Write down what you want in terms that convey the intensity of your desire.

'I must pass my exams or I won't be able to face my parents.'

'I must get my promotion or my years of hard work will be wasted.'

'If I can't have a baby I will die.'

• Now choose to let go of your desired outcome.

Put your desired outcome into the basket of a hot-air balloon. Place it there respectfully, then see it floating upwards. Soon it bumps into increasing numbers of other hot-air balloons. These all carry outcomes which may be just as beneficial. Quickly the sky is filled with bumping hot-air balloons, of every colour and size and kind you can imagine. Enjoy the sight.

• Bring your mind back to your anxiety-provoking situation.

Remind yourself about the many hot-air balloons. Resolve that whatever happens, you will observe the outcome with interest and with minimum anxiety.

This does not mean you stop studying for your exams, or looking through the employment ads, or taking advice on your fertility. It simply means you set aside your fixed idea that only a single outcome can save you.

• It may help to acknowledge that for all your certainty that you must have this, or will die without that, in fact you rarely know what an ideal outcome might be, nor what new opportunity an apparent disappointment will allow.

You fail to get a job. *It leaves you free to try for something better, or to rethink your priorities.*

Your son doesn't win a scholarship. *Perhaps he will do better and be happier in a less competitive school.*

Your partner's pathology tests confirm cancer. *Cancer is not always life-threatening but it is almost always life-changing—often necessarily.*

Your lover storms out for absolutely the last time. *Now is the time to begin grieving for a relationship that existed only in your own desires.*

• Return often to review these steps in anxiety-provoking situations. Anxiety is an excessively persistent habit (as I know only too well!). It will strenuously resist attempts to dislodge it, but the image of a sky filled to the edges of the horizon with bumping hot-air balloons has its own power too. Use it!

Not wanting—having!

Here is an irresistible encouragement to be alive in the present. Notice how your energy changes when you move from the waiting mode of the first statement to the active, assertive mode of the second.

• Identify what it is that you want, then rewrite the lines below to describe your individual situation.

• Once you are happy with your affirmation (and you might continue to change it as your wants change) then use it to the full. Sing it. Stamp it out around the room. Bellow it. Roar it. Whisper it. Confess it. Caress it. Write it on pieces of paper and paste them around the room or rip them into tiny pieces and send them out into moving water and your wishes with them.

I want to be loved. *I am loving*.
I wanted to be admired. *I am admiring*.
I want to be strong. *I am strengthening*.
I want to be desired. *I am desiring*.
I want to be wise. *I am wise*.
I want to be generous. *I am generous*.
I want to be beautiful. *I am beautiful*.
I want to sing like an angel. *I am singing like an angel*.
I want to be sexual. *I am sexual*.
I want to be noticed. *I am noticing*.
I want to be special. *I am special*.

Applying the magical balm

Do you long to have your emotional or physical aches and pains eased?

Use this sensual way to nurture yourself. Whether you are standing, sitting or lying, whether you are alone with your eyes closed or densely packed between people in a bus or train, you can move your awareness to the part of yourself that needs it most, do some healing breathing and apply the magical balm.

• Does your awareness always need to be in your head? Take time to shift your awareness to your heart, your aching back, to your sore feet, to your tense belly, to your curled fingertips, to your cold toes.

• Rest your awareness in the place that needs it most.
  Breathe in loving healing to that place.
  Feel the healing relax the tissues, ease the tension.
  Breathe out slowly, calmly.

• As that part of yourself is soothed and becomes receptive, imagine applying a small amount of magical healing balm. This balm smells and feels wonderful, and will continue the work of healing you have begun with your healing breathing.

Allow yourself time to enjoy the smell of the balm, and how it feels to the touch.

Continue to apply the balm for as long as you want.

• As you leave that needy part of yourself, promise to return soon—and do so. Regular trips of awareness around your body can give you a renewed sense of your liveliness and power.

Journey through your body

Here is a way to explore your sexual expression, the way you feel about your genitals, and also your heart and emotions. Take time to prepare for this journey of discovery. You can record the instructions, spoken slowly. Have your journal beside you and note what you are discovering. Write more fully after the meditation is over. Anita's experience given at the end might inspire you.

(If you want to work further with your sexuality, your physical body or chakras—including the solar plexus—Lucy Goodison's *Moving Heaven and Earth* is an excellent guide.)

• Close your eyes, slow your breathing: in, out; in, out. Now relax your shoulders, neck, head, tongue. Feel where your body is supported on the chair or floor. Enjoy that support. Take a couple of deep breaths into your belly. Relax your belly. Tell yourself you are taking some time away from your regular concerns to journey through your body.

• When you are ready, see an image of your physical self become smaller, smaller, smaller. When that image is really tiny, it will go inside you. This will feel comfortable and safe.

• Has that happened now? Take your time, but when that tiny you is inside your body, be aware you will see a door in your mind's eye. Look at the door, noting what kind of door it is. You may want to write down what kind of door it is, or simply remember.

It will be possible for you to open your eyes for a few seconds without losing the thread of this meditation.

• As you look even more intently now at the door, you will see words written there: the words direct you towards your sexual feelings. See those words. Notice how they are written and whether they are easy or difficult to read. *Take your time.*

• Are you ready to push open the door, and take your exploring further? If so, notice how easy or difficult it is to open the door, and what you feel as you do that. Notice whether there is any colour or smell you are aware of, or any tension in your body that you need to pause and attend to. *Take your time.*

• On the other side of the door are some steps which will take you down further, further, further into your body and further, further into your sexual feelings. Take as much time as you need to notice how it feels to go deep into your body, and to come right up close to your sexual feelings.

What are you aware of as you come closer to your sexual feelings? There may be things that are easy for you to notice. Jot down what those are. There may be things that you will be aware of more slowly. *Take your time.* Not everything needs to be noticed at once. Trust that what you do discover you will be able to work with later, and come to understand. Write down whatever you need to. These questions may help you. Ask them slowly. Be patient as you wait for answers.

Is there anything your sexual feelings want from you?

Is there anything they need?

Is there anything your genitals want from you?

Is there anything they need?

Even if you cannot meet the need at once, be respectful of it, note it down and trust that you will find a creative way to think about it.

• Send love to your sexual feelings; then to your genitals. This love is golden, the colour of healing.

• When you are ready to move on, say goodbye, knowing you can return whenever you want.

• Now, with the freedom of movement your tiny size allows, move at your own pace to your solar plexus. This is about a hand's width above your navel. The solar plexus is a storehouse for your energies and strong feelings.

Take your time here. Ask your solar plexus if there is any feeling you have been ignoring or downplaying that needs attention or releasing.

Is there any other learning that your solar plexus is ready to share? Sit quietly for a few minutes, eyes closed, breathing in to your solar plexus area, and out again. Your answer may be a word or an image. Accept whatever comes. Don't analyse it now.

Is there tension, a sense of old pain, or of things being held in which may be better expressed and brought into the open? Again, just listen with an open mind to what this part of your body is ready to tell you.

Now ask the solar plexus if there is anything else *it needs from you*. Jot down what you learn.

Perhaps your solar plexus has something to say to your genitals?

Perhaps your solar plexus has something to say to your sexuality?

Take your time to listen and learn.

• When you are ready, say goodbye to the solar plexus, knowing you can return at any time but that now your tiny, highly mobile self will move upwards through your body to the heart.

This is a time for being with your heart, and for listening to whatever your heart wants to tell you. As you listen, with an open mind, be ready to write down what you discover, then, with eyes closed, to return to your heart area to listen again.

Perhaps your heart has something to say to your genitals.

Perhaps your heart has something to say to your solar plexus.

Perhaps your heart has something to say to your self.

Is there anything your heart needs?

Listen, eyes closed, and write when you need to. Be patient and thankful for whatever your discoveries are, however tentative.

• When you are ready, move your awareness back through your body, back to your solar plexus, back to your genitals, back to the steps up which you now ascend, then to the door which you open, then close gently behind you, and now you are ready to say goodbye to your tiny self and slowly, slowly, to move your awareness back to your body as it is, full size, sitting in your room. *Take your time.*

• Now open your eyes, look around you, remind yourself where you are, take some big breaths, in, out, and stretch.

Finally, anchor your experience by writing your impressions of the journey in your journal.

Here is what Anita wrote. A dynamic, apparently successful woman, Anita believes she uses her sexuality to boost her feelings of personal power but is often left feeling sad and lonely after sexual encounters.

'I became very small and walked down towards the area of my sexual feelings. The door I saw was very old, heavy wood, but on it was a lively strip, airbrushed with clouds, and on that was written: To my sexuality. At first it felt warm, red, spacious and comfortable. The sound was a heart beat. The smell was clean vagina smell. I felt good, but as I went down the steps and deeper inside I saw there was also pain there, I tried to comfort the pain and the message I got was that it is a real shame to use my sexuality as a punishment area.

'On to the solar plexus and I got extraordinary "energy pictures" of the tiny me jumping on a trampoline! Very powerful. The message here is to acquaint myself more thoroughly with this region, to jump in, and that will give me more energy that I need.

'On up to the heart which was encrusted with what seemed like growths: warts or scars. Not at all pretty. Later I felt they were scars but deep. I wanted to see the heart grow freer of them and its health to show through more.

'I took my heart down to dialogue with my sexuality. I felt there was a strong connection between them—that they need much more flow and that if I work with my sexuality *from the heart* I will be much better off. I must be very careful not to use my sexuality to appease an anxiety. My pain should trust me more. My sexuality sometimes holds me back, but perhaps in a good way. I think I need to feel I have more choice.'

When sexual desire fades or dies

I desire you. You no longer desire me.

You desire me. I no longer desire you.

I am hurt. I withdraw. You desire me less.

You are angry. You shout. I desire you less.

Neither of us is getting our relationship needs met.

Both of us begin to doubt our capacity to love and to be loved.

It is difficult to describe what we are feeling without blaming and wanting to lash out.

But can I be blamed for no longer desiring you?

Is it fair of me to be angry with you for no longer desiring me?

Perhaps I still love you. Then why don't I desire you?

And when I say I no longer desire you, what precisely do I mean?

The apparent end of sexual desire can indicate many things in a relationship, not all of them fatal!

• If this is a current issue for you, take time to write out the list that follows, and anything else that occurs to you.

• Circle three statements which seem especially urgent or painful. Don't censor yourself, but allow plenty of time to explore them.

I am too tired to feel like sex.

The way you show your sexual feelings turns me off.

I feel invaded or overwhelmed by you when we have sex.

I feel over-connected with you and stopping sex gains me some distance.

I feel distanced and bored when we have sex.

I am weary of my own anxieties and failures around sex.

I am wearied by your anxieties and failures.

Our sexual rhythms seem disconnected: you want sex when I don't; I want sex when you don't.

I like to have sex with people I hardly know. Then I can get turned on by my fantasies about how great they are—and how great I am in their eyes.

I need a high level of excitement to overcome my inhibitions.

I need to be anxious/highly aroused/excited by novelty before I can have an orgasm.

I believe sex is dirty, dangerous, addictive.

I believe sex makes you vulnerable.

I don't like having sex in the same house where my children sleep.

I can't have sex when I am wracked with anxieties about my paid work.

Sex is one demand too many in my day.

Sex is the only way we get physically close and that makes me angry.

You over-emphasise sex and that crushes my interest.

I stopped desiring you when we stopped talking and sharing.

• Take a large sheet of paper for each of the three statements you want to explore. Write one statement on the top of each sheet. When your statements are spread around you, begin to muse on them, stopping often to go inside yourself to see what information is emerging. Then draw or write that down, before going inside once more.

Spend at least half an hour withdrawing, writing; withdrawing, writing.

• As you look over what you have written, you may feel you want to ask your partner to discuss the issues with you.

Give your partner the chance to prepare by also doing this active meditation.

If you are both willing, it will help to review Speak for yourself (see p 200) and Intimate listening (see p 196).

• If you fear that you are likely to become upset or angry in such a discussion, prepare yourself. Ask your Wise Being (see p 23) for a talisman, a Cloak of Courage, or some other protective image.

Draw the image and have it beside you as a reminder. Use aware breathing to keep your mind focused: 'Breathing in I calm my body . . .'

• Begin the discussion free of a desired agenda. Allow yourself to be surprised.

Take time for a few quiet moments of slowed-down breathing together before you begin.

• Whatever the outcome, there may be some painful feelings aired. These meditations can support you, individually and together.

Meditating on the self of the other (see p 159).

Trade-offs (see p 179).

Too many demands (see p 186).

I am no longer sexually desiring

When you are no longer desiring your partner sexually, it can be one of several possible indicators that a relationship is not working (high levels of friction, poor communication, increased dependence on drugs or alcohol, depression, sleeplessness, boredom, having or planning sex with other partners can also be danger signals). It may cause a crisis painful enough to wonder what this relationship means to you, what you want in general from your partner; from relationships; from life.

This meditation will help you reflect on what is happening. You will almost certainly need to carry it over several sessions. A lot is asked of you here.

• Write out all the questions below, and any others that occur to you.

• When you have finished, take time to choose any that seem to demand attention. Write each on its own large sheet of paper.

Take at least fifteen minutes to explore the question: thinking, writing or drawing; withdrawing to think some more; writing. Some questions might disturb you. It is important to move slowly.

• Note particularly your *emotional* responses and resistances, and if there is a gap between what you *should* think and what you *do* feel. Watch your breathing, and for tension in your body. Note that down.

What needs do I believe should be met in a sexual relationship? (These needs do not have to be reasonable. Put them all down, no matter how outrageous. This is a process of discovery.)

Could those needs be met within this relationship other than through sex?

Could those needs be met in other non-sexual relationships?

Have I overloaded this relationship with expectations from the past?

Have I been in this non-desiring role before? Always? Do I have any sense as to why this is my role?

Is my partner asking me to parent her as well as be her lover (see p 167)? How do I feel about that?

By withholding sex, what am I saying to my partner?

By withholding sex, or having sex only under sufferance, what am I saying about the way I feel about myself?

What has changed from the time when I did feel desiring until now? Could any of those earlier conditions be reclaimed? (These might include time, privacy, a sense of occasion, tender nurturance out of bed.)

Does not having sex give me the emotional separateness I need?

Am I angry with my partner? Can I say that directly (see p 80)?

Am I grieving?

What is the tone of this relationship in general? How would I describe it with one adjective or image only?

Is contraception a worrying issue for me, or failing to get pregnant?

Do I trust my partner?

Am I disappointed by how different my partner is from the person I had in my fantasy?

Am I addicted to new sex, dangerous sex, unfamiliar sex? Do I know why?

Do I need sex to be more tender than it is, more varied, more experimental, or more reassuring? Do I know what I want? Can I tell my partner what I want?

What difference would it make if I could decide when and how we have sex?

What do I gain from not desiring my partner? (More power within the relationship; greater autonomy; a chance to punish the other person or a way of decreasing dependence?)

Do I know how I want to express my deepest self sexually, if at all? What image can my eternal world supply to help me understand this?

What image would help me understand what stands between me and an ideal expression of sexuality in this relationship?

Would I desire differently in another relationship? Could I bring those missing elements to this relationship?

Could I make any small change in myself to have the relationship I want?

• Only when you feel you understand as much as you can, should you ask your partner if she or he is willing to discuss this issue with you. Follow the steps given in the previous active meditation.

I am no longer sexually desired

It can feel crushing to be in a sexual relationship, but not be desired. Yet the situation may be much more complicated, on *both* sides, than one person 'going off' the other.

Take it for granted that when your partner ceases to be desiring, there is a great deal going on—much of which may have nothing to do with you and may persist from a time when your relationship did not even exist. It can be helpful to decentralise yourself from the drama (see p 185), at least until the limits of your endurance are within sight.

Then, when you feel you must act, choose to act on your own behalf, remembering, *You cannot change another person; you can only change your attitude towards them.*

• Explore this issue slowly over several sessions, using the following questions to prompt you to think outside the circles in which your mind may have been turning.

Write out all the questions, and any others that may occur to you. Then choose those that seem most urgent to you.

• Write those questions out, one on each separate sheet of paper. Take time to hold the question in your mind, muse on it, then write; withdraw to think, write. Take at least fifteen minutes for each question and keep all the sheets spread around you. As you explore one question, you may want to return to another.

• Monitor your breathing, and any tension in your body. Note, too, your emotional responses and where or how they are in conflict with your belief systems. (I know I shouldn't feel this but . . . I have always thought . . . yet now I find myself acting . . .)

How do I feel about not being desired in this relationship?

What does being desired mean to me?

Is this a familiar situation? Have I been 'not-desired' in other relationships? Is there a pattern that it would be useful to think about?

Does my partner no longer desire me at all, or is the desiring less frequent or direct than I would like?

Do I still feel loved?

Is my partner physically loving in non-sexual ways?

Have I been asking my partner to take care of me where I could take care of myself (see pp 153, 172)?

Have I been bullying or tyrannising my partner, or making her or him feel small or ashamed?

Have I changed in any major way from the person my partner once desired?

What is the general temperature of the relationship?

Are there aspects of the relationship still working well?

Are we able to speak to each other about what we feel?

What is going on in the life of my partner that wasn't present when desiring seemed easier?

Is my partner ill or grieving, depressed or anxious?

What stresses or anxieties might prevent my partner from wanting sex?

Do I know what sex means to my partner, what emotions it is intended to carry?

What do I want from sex? (Emotional closeness, physical release, confirmation of my desirability, cementing of the relationship?)

What are my partner's reasons for not having sex? (Write them all down.)

Can I accept that sex may be more important to me than to my partner and that sex is my own responsibility? (Could you masturbate for sexual release, or have other partners? Perhaps what you want from sex can be experienced in non-sexual ways: dancing, massage, cuddling, increasing self-acceptance.)

Can I talk about sex without getting angry and demanding?

Have I tried some gentle wooing?

Could I give my partner the power to decide when we will have sex?

Could I develop more non-sexual relationships?

Could I tone down my feelings about sex and being desired from an addiction to a preference (see p 238)?

Do I know what the limits are to what I can tolerate?

Do I risk losing this relationship if I state my limits?

If I am never desired by this person again, do I want to continue with the relationship?

If I want to continue, what small change would make the situation tolerable for me?

• As with the two preceding active meditations, these questions can lead to a considerable increase in self-knowledge, and may even relieve the situation without discussion becoming necessary.

If you want to discuss the issue with your partner, take time to prepare (see p 200). Bear in mind that your feelings of rejection may be matched by your partner's feelings of loss (of desire, sexual energy, commitment or even of self-love). This knowledge may not lessen your pain, but can help you understand how any discussion of the topic could remind two people they both feel wounded. The less 'punished' your partner feels, the more fruitful the discussion is likely to be.

Reversing roles

It can be surprisingly enlightening to take up the questions suggested in either of the two preceding active meditations *as though you were your partner*. (If you are not desiring, consider the questions to the desiring partner. Or vice versa.)

• Take time to get into the thinking, feeling and attitudes of your partner. This will help you see where there is an uncomfortable push-me/pull-you tussle going on; where one partner is expressing a difficulty on behalf of both; where you may be closer to understanding and negotiating than you think.

• Write whatever you discover in your journal, going back repeatedly into the mind and feelings of your partner, looking for insights. Do not necessarily or immediately share those insights with your partner! ('Now I know what you think, darling . . .')

Give yourself time to untangle your own projections, wishes and even feelings of hostility, which may be confusing the issues.

• If you and your partner are still on relatively good terms, do this exercise separately.

Take time (at least a week) to consider your discoveries. Then come together to talk, following the intimate listening practices outlined on pp 196, 197. You may also want to meditate on shared symbols (see p 160), but do so only when there is still loving energy flowing between you.

Giving sexual desire the kiss of life

When the desire to love and be loved is still present, it is possible to reawaken sexual desire within a long-term relationship—though it may reappear in a different garb.

Sometimes this depends on good luck. Something shifts: a child begins to sleep through the night; financial burdens ease; chronic ill-health gives way to health; retirement from paid work offers fresh possibilities. Conscious awareness—as in all troubling situations—will also be a powerful ally, for the less pressure there is on a sexual relationship the more it is likely to flourish. Remember: sexual love is important to many people, maybe most, but it is not the only way to express warmth, appreciation and affection.

Enlarging your circle of relationships and spreading your willingness to be loving (see p 167) powerfully decreases your dependency on one less-than-ideal relationship.

Enlarging the circle of pleasure you and your partner can enjoy, separately and together, also takes the strain out of sex as the major compensation for an often harsh, even brutal world outside the home.

There are many programmes offered by marriage and sex therapists to heterosexual and gay couples seeking to revive their sex life. These usually take the emphasis off genital sex, and build up from wooing and massage to body appreciation and only gradually to genital sex again. Such programmes have a strong record of success, but I would suggest taking the focus even further away from genital activity, and waking up your joy in being alive. Then whether sex happens, how often it happens and whether it lights up the sky becomes increasingly irrelevant (and sometimes increasingly easy; but that's a by-product, not a goal).

• See your situation as a joint creative challenge to revive the sense of aliveness and mutual pleasure that once made sex easy, made laughing easy and made the world seem a wonderful place.

Take time to remember and identify all the things you have or once had in common with your partner, and that you could both enjoy doing. Write those down.

Maybe there are things that only one of you enjoys, but the other could share. Write those down as sources of possible trade-offs (see p 179).

Note what you could be doing with other people that would bring you home to your partner stimulated, interested, relaxed.

When you are able to unravel your lack of desire back to a certain point, ask yourself if that pre-condition could be momentarily revived, not to have sex, to have *fun*. (This might mean getting together with people who appreciate you; going for a walk somewhere beautiful; playing old music you can sing along to, and dancing in the kitchen!)

Check out how much time you give to listening, talking and relaxing (remember, you are forgetting about sex). If it is the ragged end of the day, every day, and neither of you can remember when you last had fun, see if your partner would be willing to explore What matters in your life (see p 112). There are always adjustments that can be made, even in the most crowded schedule. (Why is that schedule so crowded anyway?)

Giving and receiving gifts may not revive sexual interest, but it can signify that each person is thinking of the other, and wanting to enhance their life. Those gifts need not be purchased. An extra hour in bed, an offer to massage tired feet or run a bath; a willingness to be silent rather than critical (see pp 80, 107); wearing clothes your partner especially likes; help with a regular chore; words of appreciation written down and decorated: these can all lighten a day, and a heart.

Be vigilant about not 'dumping' on the other person. Venting your frustrations, your self-hatred or your lack of self-respect on the unfortunate person who is sharing your life is a certain killer of tenderness. Be sure you are *at least* as considerate of your partner as you are of people at the outer edges of your intimacy circles.

• Patterns of life that exclude having fun, relaxing, taking time to appreciate each other, can be hard to shake. When you and your partner have set up a fun strategy, a sharing strategy or a life-force strategy, you will need to monitor it often.

Resolve to support each other. When slip-ups inevitably happen, see them not as a predictable disappointment or failure, but as a jolt to your joint creativity.

This too will change.

Reviewing your day

'By keeping a diary of what made me happy I had discovered that happiness came when I was most widely aware . . . And, by finding that in order to be more and more aware I had to be more and more still, I had not only come to see through my own eyes instead of at second hand, but I had also finally come to discover what was the way of escape from the imprisoning island of my own self-consciousness.'

Marion Milner, *A Life of One's Own*

• Create the habit of reviewing your day. Start with the evening and roll the day backwards, ending at the moment when you woke.

If this is difficult to do at first, simply imagine that you are observing your life as though it were someone else's—a someone who deeply interests you and for whom you feel compassion, but not pity.

• Note in your journal the moments of the day when you felt most yourself (and perhaps happiest, or most real) and those moments when you felt least yourself (and perhaps least happy or least real).

Soon you will see a pattern to these times. You can then begin to know what does bring you happiness or satisfaction, and make more of those times.

Choose to bring more awareness to the unhappy times—not to dwell on them but to shift their emphasis in some small but crucial way. ('These are the times I like least, but they are part of a larger pattern.' 'These are the times I feel most stressed, I am working to minimise these contacts.')

It can even help simply to resolve to bring your awareness to such moments: *this too will pass.*

Likewise, with your happier or more real moments: *I am at this moment content—and grateful for that. This too will pass. And will come around again.*

• You can deepen your practice by deciding on a reminder that will bring your awareness into the present: as the clock strikes; each time you replace the receiver on your phone; when the dog barks; when your children call out 'Mum'; as you enter or leave your home, or pass through a particular doorway (which you can decorate as your 'doorway to awareness').

Reviewing the day with children

Taking some quiet moments to review the day with your child can be helpful to the child and instructive and connecting for the parent. It is best done before the child sleeps when she (or he) is already cosy in bed. The reviewing can simply focus on a happy and an unhappy moment or episode. Review the unhappy moment first, then move on to the happy moment.

• 'Tell me about the worst moment of your day? Was there one?' (Many children feel unconsciously forbidden to share anything but triumphs. Are you aware of that?)

DO NOT engage in a discussion as to whether your child's unhappiness is justified or legitimate. The feeling belongs to the child, not to you. Keep your comments to a neutral minimum: 'That must have been hard.' 'I see what you mean.' 'Goodness me, what a day!'

• 'Tell me what you enjoyed most today. Was there a lovely moment today?'

If there was no lovely moment at all, accept that, but express your wish that tomorrow will be a much better day. Affirm your child's capacity and entitlement to pleasure: 'I feel sure a lovely moment is waiting just for you.'

When your child can tell you what made her happy, again avoid long discussions, but she will be glad to see that you are listening empathically, giving your full attention to what is being said and responding to the mood even more than to the words or content. (There is more about aware listening on pp 197.)

• If what your child tells you distresses her, ask her if she would like time to discuss the issue tomorrow, if it still feels like a problem when she wakes up. Bedtime is not a good time to get into heavy problem-solving.

If what your child tells you distresses *you*, take it as a problem to your Wise Being (see p 23) or Eternal Mother (see p 120). Ask for the help you need.

• the simple meditation on love (see p 221) is a wonderful way to drift into sleep, for children as well as for adults.

Listening. Just Listening.

This is self-therapy in its simplest and most powerful form. It comes from Ingram Smith's account of his journey with Krishnamurti, *Truth is a Pathless Land*.

'I have had it wrong all my life. I've been looking for improvement, change for the better. Whenever I noticed something painful, foolish or false I worked at ways to improve the situation or to change myself. At four o'clock one morning I awoke and knew that this process, acceptable in the physical world, is utterly meaningless in the inner world.

'What I actually saw was: *Stop whatever I am doing the moment I am aware that it is not true*. That is all. No positive action whatsoever.

"The implications are vast. First, the negation of the false is wholly positive because it is immediately finished, there and then. No time is needed to correct the error. There is no changing this for that; no thought for the future that "I will not make this mistake again."

'While the unwanted is held in mind so that it can be seen, understood and hopefully resolved, the problem is being sustained. To try to stop thinking about something is impossible because I have to keep it in mind in order to remember not to think about it, and thereby keeping alive what I want to forget. Clearly the critical point is the moment I am aware there is a disturbance. For example, the instant I sense I am overeating, to stop. Or if I catch myself exaggerating or lying, to pause and listen. On noticing anger rising, to wait and watch. Perception alone dictating, directing, letting go.

'Given no energy, the false atrophies. Living takes on a new freedom. I find myself listening, not to outside noises or for guidance, not to inward thoughts and feelings. Just listening. Not to learn about myself and life gradually, through time, at my convenience. Listening. Just listening.'

• Spend several sessions doing nothing more demanding than reading this passage, writing it out, musing on it, allowing it to work for you. If specific thoughts, or modest resolutions, occur to you, note them in your journal.

• As you begin to follow the practice, use your journal as an ally, noting your successes and also when 'Just listening' is difficult, not to chastise yourself, but to bring renewed awareness and self-support to those moments.

Measure your life with a piece of string

'The meaning and value of a human life do not lie in any one isolated moment, but in a process which unfolds, at the very least, between physical birth and death.'

Roberto Assagioli,
'Symbols of Transpersonal Experiences'

• Cut a piece of string. It can be as long or as short as you want.
  See one end as representing your birth, and the other representing your death.
• Spend some quiet time simply holding that piece of string and being with it. When you feel ready to do so, tie a knot in the string at a place which seems to represent the point in your life *where you are now* (somewhere between birth and death).
• Use this knot to keep you awake to your choices: about the way you are living, how you are expressing your deepest self; how alive you are to others: your immediate circle, the larger circle of humankind.
• Think about your choices. Write about them in your journal.
• Return to look at the string, to finger the knot.
  Value the here, the now, and who you are.
• Choose wakefulness.
• Be thankful.

Conscious choosing

'To get we must also give, to advance we must surrender, to gain we must lose, to attain we must resign. From the nature of things life means choice and selection, and every positive choice negates all other possibilities.'

Rufus Jones in *Daily Readings from Quaker Spirituality*

You have come so far. Or is this where you are beginning?
• Allow conscious choosing to become part of your mindfulness:

'I am making choices ... "every positive choice negates all other possibilities."'

And who is making those choices?

It is your self: a self like no other; a self in constant relationship with others.

Wanting to find a way to express how important this relatedness is, and searching for a passionate endorsement that self-therapy can most decidedly open you up to the world outside yourself as much as it reveals to you your own inner richness, I came across the following quote. The writer, Frances Vaughan, is talking here about intuition, which is one aspect only of self-therapy, but her lines express the exact thought I want to leave you with.

'Working on oneself and developing intuition are not alternatives to working in the world. Nor are they substitutes for rational faculties. On the contrary, they lead to a recognition that one is capable of both intuitive *and* rational ways of knowing.'

In other words, one is — we all are — capable of striving for self-understanding and self-responsibility *and* of being alive to all the other urgent issues that must and should concern us. It is inconceivable that one kind of knowledge and activity has a valid existence without the other.

'If one tries to change society without changing consciousness, one is simply rearranging the contents of experience. If one works exclusively on consciousness and abdicates social responsibility, one separates oneself from the world and again falls into the trap of identifying with a part instead of the whole. Like breathing in and breathing out, one needs both activity and receptivity. Exclusive emphasis on either mode becomes an imbalance. Awakening intuition [doing self-therapy] depends on your willingness to see things as they really are, to know yourself as you really are, and to see the world as it really is, with all the beauty and all the suffering. Intuition [self-therapy] deepens the experience of life in all its facets.'

Frances E. Vaughan, *Awakening Intuition*

Hope is the thing with feathers—
That perches in the soul—
And sings the tune without the words—
And never stops—at all—

Further reading

(Details in the Bibliography)

Jean Dalby Clift and Wallace B. Clift, *Symbols of Transformation in Dreams*

Sheila Ernst & Lucy Goodison, *In Our Own Hands: A Book of Self-Help Therapy*

Piero Ferrucci, *What We May Be: The Visions and Techniques of Psychosynthesis*

Lucy Goodison, *Moving Heaven and Earth: Sexuality, Spirituality and Social Change*

Thich Nhat Hanh, *Peace Is Every Step: The Path of Mindfulness in Everyday Life*

Bibliography

Assagioli, Roberto, *Psychosynthesis, a Manual of Principles and Techniques*, Hobbs Doorman, New York, 1965.

Bancroft, Anne, *Weavers of Wisdom: Women Mystics of the 20th Century*, Arkana, London, 1989.

Blanchard, Brand, in Cell, E. (ed), inf.

Cell, E. (ed), *Daily Readings from Quaker Spirituality*, Templegate Publishers, Springfield, Ill. 1987.

Clift, Jean Dalby and Clift, Wallace B., *Symbols of Transformation in Dreams*, Collins Dove, Blackburn, Vic., 1989 (also Crossroad Publishing, New York).

Colegrave, Sukie, *The Spirit of the Valley*, Virago, London, 1979.

Craighead, Meinrad, 'Immanent Mother' in Giles, M. (ed), inf.

Davis, Noël, 'One with Love's Silent Song' from *The Heart That Goes Walkabout*, Shekinah Creative Ministry, Sydney, 1991.

Deikman, Arthur J., *The Observing Self*, Beacon Press, Boston, 1982.

Dowrick, Stephanie, *Running Backwards Over Sand*, Viking, Harmondsworth & Melbourne, 1985.

——, *Intimacy and Solitude*, Wm Heinemann Australia, Melbourne, 1991; The Women's Press, London, 1992.

Edmond, Lauris, *Selected Poems*, O.U.P., Auckland, 1984.

Ernst, Sheila, & Goodison, Lucy, *In Our Own Hands: A Book of Self-Help Therapy*, The Women's Press, London, 1981.

Ferrucci, Piero, *What We May Be: The Visions and Techniques of Psychosynthesis*, Turnstone, Wellingborough, 1982.

Frankl, Viktor E., *The Will to Meaning*, Souvenir Press, London, 1971.

Franz, Marie-Louise von, *Carl Gustav Jung: His Myth in Our Time*, G. P. Putnam's Sons, New York, 1975.

Furlong, Monica, *Genuine Fake: A Biography of Alan Watts*, Wm Heinemann, London, 1986.

Giles, Mary E. (ed), *The Feminist Mystic and Other Essays on Women and Spirituality*, Crossroad Publishing, New York, 1982.

Goldberg, Natalie, *Wild Mind: Living the Writer's Life*, Bantam, New York, 1990.

Goldberg, P., *The Intuitive Edge*, Turnstone, Wellingborough, 1985.

Goodison, Lucy, *Moving Heaven and Earth: Sexuality, Spirituality and Social Change*, The Women's Press, London, 1990.

Hall, Nor, *The Moon and the Virgin: Reflections on the Archetypal Feminine*, The Women's Press, London, 1980.

Hanh, Thich Nhat, *Peace Is Every Step: The Path of Mindfulness in Everyday Life*, Bantam, New York, 1991.

Haronian, Frank, 'The Repression of the Sublime,' in Fadiman, James (ed), *The Proper Study of Man*, Macmillan, New York, 1971.

Hobson, Robert F., *Forms of Feeling: The Heart of Psychotherapy*, Tavistock, London, 1985.

Jones, Rufus, in Cell, E. (ed) v. sup.

Jung, C. G., *Memories, Dreams and Reflections*, Routledge & Kegan Paul, London, 1963.

Keyes, Ken, Jr., *A Conscious Person's Guide to Relationships*, Love Line Books, Oregon, 1979.

Khema, Ayya, *Be An Island Unto Yourself*, Parappuduwa Nuns Island, Sri Lanka, 1986.

Kober, Catherine, 'Shifting the Pavement', in *Free Associations*, 10, London, 1987.

Krishnamurti, J., *You Are the World*, Harper & Row, New York, 1972.

Lao Tzu, *Tao Te Ching*, (trans. Lau, D. C.), Penguin, Harmondsworth, 1963.

Lewis, C. S., *Mere Christianity*, Collins, London, 1952.

Lowen, Alexander, *Narcissim: Denial of the True Self*, Macmillan, New York, 1983.

——, *The Betrayal of the Body*, Macmillan, New York, 1967.

Mascaro, J. (translator), *The Dhammapada: The Path of Perfection*, Penguin, Harmondsworth, 1973.

Miller, Alice, *Breaking Down the Wall of Silence (To Join the Waiting Child)*, Virago, London, 1992.

Miles, Margaret R., 'The Courage To Be Alone—In and Out of Marriage', in Giles, Mary E. (ed), v. sup.

Milner, Marion, *A Life of One's Own*, Penguin, Harmondsworth, 1955.

O'Connor, Peter, *Dreams and the Search for Meaning*, Methuen Haynes, Sydney, 1986.

Pincus, Lily & Dare, Christopher, *Secrets in the Family*, Faber & Faber, London, 1978.

Raine, Kathleen, *Farewell Happy Fields*, Hamish Hamilton, London, 1974.

Ross, Gillian, *Yoga Nidra Relaxation* (cassette tape), ABC Audio Tapes, Sydney, 1992.

Rush, Anne Kent, *Getting Clear: Body Work for Women*, Wildwood House, London, 1974.

Samuels, M. & Samuels, N., *Seeing With the Mind's Eye*, Random House, New York, 1975.

Sharp, Daryl, *The Survival Papers: Applied Jungian Psychology*, Quantum, n.d.

Sheehy, Gail, *Passages: Predictable Crises of Adult Life*, Dutton, New York, 1976.

Siegel, Bernie S., *Love, Medicine and Miracles*, Harper & Row, New York, 1986.

Simonton, O. C., Mathews-Simonton, S. and Creighton, J., *Getting Well Again*, Bantam, New York, 1980.

Smiley, Jane, *The Age of Grief*, Knopf, New York, 1987.

Smith, Ingram, *Truth is a Pathless Land*, Quest (The Theosophical Publishing House), Wheaton, Ill., 1989.

Sohl, R. & Carr, A., *The Gospel According to Zen*, Mentor, New York, 1970.

Starhawk, *Dreaming the Dark*, Beacon, Boston, 1982.

——, *The Spiral Dance*, Harper & Row, San Francisco, 1979.

Vaughan, Frances E., *Awakening Intuition*, Anchor, New York, 1979.

Waters, F. *The Book of the Hopi*, Ballantine, New York, 1963.

Whitaker, Carl (with Napier, Augustus Y.), *The Family Crucible*, Harper & Row, New York, 1978.

Whitmore, Diana, *Psychosynthesis Counselling in Action*, Sage, London, 1991.

Yalom, Irvin D., *Existential Psychotherapy*, Basic Books, New York, 1980.

Index

The headings lead you to page numbers where you will find practical support for working with these topics. Hold your chosen topic in mind when you are moving through an active meditation or exercise. You are likely to use the same meditation to explore different topics. Each time your emphasis will shift and your experience will deepen. Do not limit yourself to my suggestions. Your intuition and creativity will allow you to reshape the meditations for your own needs.